BLOOM CREEK
quilts

Vicki Bellino

Martingale®
& COMPANY

Credits

President & CEO: Tom Wierzbicki
Editor in Chief: Mary V. Green
Managing Editor: Tina Cook
Developmental Editor: Karen Costello Soltys
Technical Editor: Ellen Pahl
Copy Editor: Marcy Heffernan
Design Director: Stan Green
Production Manager: Regina Girard
Illustrators: Adrienne Smitke & Robin Strobel
Cover & Text Designer: Shelly Garrison
Photographer: Brent Kane

Mission Statement

Dedicated to providing quality
products and service to inspire creativity.

Bloom Creek Quilts
© 2010 by Vicki Bellino

That Patchwork Place® is an imprint of
Martingale & Company®.

Martingale & Company
20205 144th Ave. NE
Woodinville, WA 98072-8478 USA
www.martingale-pub.com

Printed in China
15 14 13 12 11 10   8 7 6 5 4 3 2 1

Library of Congress Cataloging-in-Publication Data is available upon request.

ISBN: 978-1-60468-002-7

DEDICATION

To Anne Myers—my forever friend . . .
because of quilting.

34

58

86

CONTENTS

38

64

96

INTRODUCTION

As I began to work on this book, I knew I wanted to include a variety of projects—some small, some larger, some with appliqué and some without, some made using traditional fabrics, some with a more contemporary look, some made with precuts, as well as a few new designs. That's when it dawned on me why I'm so passionate about quilting. Quilting affords us so very many choices! From patterns to fabrics, from notions to thread, from tools to techniques, there's something out there for everyone.

I enjoyed choosing projects to include in this book, and it gave me the opportunity to remake a few of my older designs, making changes that were either a result of requests by customers, or my own "shoulda, coulda, wouldas," such as enlarging quilts or converting a design from Charm Packs or Jelly Rolls to yardage.

I choose to make and machine quilt the majority of my quilts, but when time is a factor, I'm fortunate to have the option of sending out the piecing to Susan Armington, whom I call the perfect piecer! For machine quilting, I turn my quilt tops over to Veronica Nurmi, an extraordinary quilter who also taught me how to machine quilt. I designed, pieced, and quilted all of the quilts in this book, unless otherwise stated.

Creativity is what quilting is all about, which is why I'm a firm believer that there is no right or wrong way in quilting, but rather the way that works best for you. I've provided a few of my favorite techniques. That doesn't mean they're the "right way" to do things, but they work best for me. I encourage you to experience a variety of techniques by either taking classes or joining quilting groups; you'll not only find the techniques that are most comfortable for you, but you'll develop lifelong friends who share your enthusiasm for quilting!

There are many methods and techniques for just about any aspect of quilting. I believe there's no right or wrong way, and I'll share the techniques that work best for me. If you prefer a different technique to achieve the same result, use it!

With that said, I do believe there's one constant in quiltmaking, and that is an accurate ¼" seam allowance. All of the projects in this book are made using a ¼" seam allowance, unless otherwise indicated. Test the accuracy of your seam allowance before beginning a project. You can do this by sewing two 2" squares together. Press the seam allowances to one side and measure the unit; it should measure 2" x 3½". If it doesn't, adjust your seam allowance until you achieve the correct measurement.

WORKING WITH PRECUT FABRICS

I thoroughly enjoy designing and quilting with precut fabrics such as Charm Squares and Jelly Rolls. Charm Squares are 5" x 5" and come in packs of 25 to 40 or more. Jelly Rolls are 2½" x 42" strips that come rolled together in fun bundles. They're a time-saver, since the squares and strips are already cut and the fabric selection has already been made. However, as there are many times when these might not be available in your local quilt shop, you can always convert Charm Squares and Jelly Rolls to yardage.

   8 Charm Squares = ¼ yard

   9 to 12 Charm Squares = 1 fat quarter

Example: If a pattern calls for 40 Charm Squares, you'll need four to five fat quarters, or five ¼-yard cuts. While you will have approximately the same amount of fabric, there will be less variety than the assortment of Charm Squares, and your quilt will have a less scrappy look.

   3 Jelly Roll strips = ¼ yard

Note: Fat quarters can be substituted if the pattern doesn't require you to use the full length of the 42" strip.

Several of the projects in this book give you the choice of using either precut fabrics or yardage for specific parts of the quilt.

APPLIQUÉ

Just when I thought I had quiltmaking down, I was introduced to appliqué. It has added a whole new dimension to my quilts. I enjoy it so much, because the process is very relaxing and the result is rewarding. Initially, I only did hand appliqué, but as time became a factor, I ventured into machine appliqué, and then to fusible appliqué. Once again, I have choices for the technique that will work best for a particular project.

You, too, can choose the technique you prefer. You'll need just a few materials and supplies for either freezer-paper appliqué or fusible appliqué.

• Freezer paper or fusible web

• Pencil

• Scissors for cutting paper

• Appliqué glue

• Monofilament or lightweight thread

• Set of bias press bars (for bias vines)

Freezer-Paper Appliqué

This method results in appliqué pieces with turned-under edges. The pieces can either be hand or machine stitched in place on the block or quilt.

1. Trace appliqué patterns onto the paper (non-shiny) side of the freezer paper. For this method of appliqué, you'll need to cut a freezer-paper template for each piece needed. For example, if there are eight leaves in the project, you'll need to cut eight leaves out of freezer paper. Using your scissors for cutting paper, cut out the shapes on the traced line.

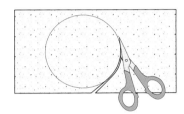

2. Iron the freezer-paper templates, shiny side down, onto the **right side** of the chosen appliqué fabric. Cut the piece out, adding a ¼" seam allowance around the entire shape. *Note: For small pieces, or those with points, a smaller seam allowance will work better.*

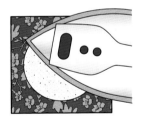 

3. Carefully peel off the freezer-paper template. Turn the fabric piece over so that the wrong side is facing up. Center the freezer paper template, with the shiny side facing up, on top of the fabric, with the ⅛" to ¼" seam allowance all around.

Using a small iron and a smooth, firm surface, iron the seam allowance over the edge of the freezer-paper template.

Mini Ironing Board

I made an appliqué pressing board using a 12" x 12" scrap of ½"-thick particle board. I covered it with silver, heat-resistant ironing-board fabric, and then used a staple gun to secure it onto the back of the board. It's portable and works great!

4. On the wrong side of the shape, apply a few small dots of appliqué glue to the seam allowance and gently finger-press the shape into position on your block or quilt, leaving the freezer paper in place.

5. To machine stitch the appliqué pieces in place, there are several options for both the thread and the stitch. If you don't want the thread to show, use monofilament (clear for light fabrics and smoke for dark) and a 60/8 machine needle. Or, you can use a fine, lightweight thread that matches the color of the appliqué fabric and a 70/10 machine needle. Use an open-toe foot for good visibility and set your machine to a blind hemstitch, or a stitch

similar to the one shown. This will result in a nearly invisible stitch. You can also use a small zigzag stitch, blanket stitch, or other decorative stitch if you want the stitching to be part of the design.

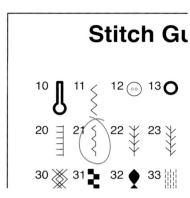

6.   Begin stitching by using a straight stitch and take a few very short stitches to anchor the thread. Change to your chosen stitch and sew around the shape carefully, slowly turning the shape as you stitch around curves. To pivot at corners and points, stop with the needle in the down position, lift the presser foot, and turn the appliqué piece. Do this when the needle is along the outer edge in the background fabric, not in the appliqué fabric. When you reach the starting point, change to a straight stitch and take a few short tacking stitches or backstitches to anchor the thread. Clip the threads and remove from the machine.

7.   Turn the quilt (or block) over and cut away the fabric inside of the appliqué stitching, leaving a ¼" seam allowance. Remove the paper. Press the piece gently from the right side.

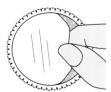

Hand Appliqué

Follow steps 1–4 of "Freezer-Paper Appliqué" on page 9 to prepare and position the appliqué pieces. Use an appliqué needle and thread that matches the fabric. Because the edges are already turned under, hand appliqué will be easy and relaxing.

Knot the thread and bring the needle up through the edge of the appliqué shape. Insert the needle into the background fabric right next to the appliqué and bring it up about ¹⁄₁₆" to ⅛" away, catching just a few threads along the folded edge of the appliqué shape. Continue around the shape until you reach the beginning stitch. Knot the thread on the wrong side of the fabric and follow step 7 of "Freezer-Paper Appliqué."

Fusible Appliqué

This method results in a raw edge, but one that's finished with machine stitching. There are many different fusible webs available on the market, but I find that a lightweight product works the best. General instructions will be provided here, but check the manufacturer's instructions beforehand for the product you use. This method is fast, but be sure to reverse the patterns, if they're not already reversed, when tracing onto the fusible web.

1.   Trace the appliqué patterns onto the paper side of the fusible web.

2.   Cut out the shapes approximately ¼" beyond the traced lines. For larger pieces, I use the "windowpane" technique and cut away the fusible web in the center, leaving approximately ¼" of web inside the traced line. Using the windowpane technique prevents stiffness and keeps the

appliqués soft and flexible, because they're not fused in the center.

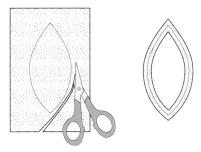

3. With the fusible side down and following the manufacturer's instructions, iron the fusible web onto the **wrong side** of the appliqué fabric. Cut out each piece on the traced lines.

 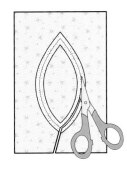 

4. Remove the paper and position the appliqué pieces onto the block (or quilt) and iron in place, following the manufacturer's instructions. Machine stitch around the raw edges with a blanket stitch, satin stitch, or invisible stitch as described in steps 5 and 6 of "Freezer-Paper Appliqué" on pages 9 and 10.

Bias Vines

There are several different methods for making bias vines, but the method below is the technique I find to be the easiest.

1. Open up the fabric so that it has no fold. Position the 45° line of an acrylic ruler on one selvage edge. Using a rotary cutter, cut along the long edge of the acrylic ruler. Move the ruler over

to the desired width of the bias strip and make another cut. Continue in this manner until the required number of strips is cut.

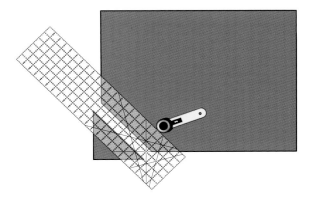

2. To make one long bias strip, sew strips together at a 45° angle along the short ends. Place strips right sides together, offsetting the ends by ¼". Sew, trim the points, and press the seam allowances open.

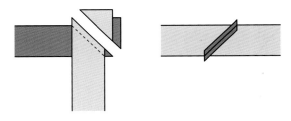

3. Fold the bias strip in half with **wrong sides** together and press. Sew ¼" from the raw edge the entire length of the bias strip.

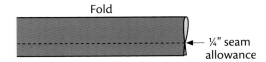

Fold

← ¼" seam allowance

4. Working on your ironing surface, insert a bias press bar (metal or plastic) into the bias strip and roll the seam allowance to the top when moving down the bias bar. Press well as you move the bias strip down the bar, pressing the seam allowances to the side. Continue until the entire strip has been pressed. (Spray sizing works well for this step.) Remove the bias bar. (*Note: If bias vines are narrow, it may be necessary to trim the seam allowances in order to keep them from showing.*)

← Bias bar

5. Use dots of appliqué glue to position the vine on the quilt top. Appliqué by hand or machine using a blind stitch, blanket stitch, or small zigzag stitch.

HALF-SQUARE-TRIANGLE UNITS

I've tried many methods for making half-square-triangle units, and it seems no matter how hard I tried, I ended up with some that were slightly smaller or slightly larger than what I wanted. Because of that, I start by cutting slightly oversized squares. After sewing and cutting, I square up the blocks to the exact unfinished size. I highly recommend a Bias Square® ruler for this. The 6" ruler will work well for most of the quilts in this book, but there's also one that requires a 9½" Bias Square ruler.

As a general rule of thumb, cut squares that are 1" larger than the size of the finished half-square-triangle unit needed. For this example, let's say that we need a 4" finished half-square-triangle unit.

1. Cut two squares, 5" x 5", one a lighter shade than the other so that you will have contrast between the pieces. Draw a diagonal line from corner to corner on the *wrong side* of the lighter square. Place the squares right sides together with the diagonal line on top and sew ¼" on each side of the line. Cut apart on the drawn line and press the seam allowances toward the darker fabric, unless otherwise indicated. This method will yield two identical half-square-triangle units.

2. Use spray sizing on each unit and press. This will keep the block nice and flat and minimize distortion when sewing.

3. Now trim the half-square-triangle unit to its unfinished size, 4½" x 4½". Place the Bias Square ruler on top of the right side of the unit, aligning the diagonal line on the ruler with the seam and lining up two sides of the unit with the 4½" marks on the ruler. Hold the ruler securely in place with your non-cutting hand, and rotary cut the remaining two sides with your dominant hand.

PREPARING FOR MACHINE QUILTING

I machine quilt most of my own projects using a home sewing machine with a longer arm and with extra length to the right of the needle. I will share the steps I use to prepare a quilt top for machine quilting. If you send your quilts out to be machine quilted, be sure to check with the quilter to determine how large the backing fabric and batting need to be.

1. Mark the quilting design onto the right side of the finished quilt top. Be sure to use a water-soluble marking pen or pencil. An assortment of these can be found at your local quilt shop.

2. Now prepare the backing fabric. If your quilt is large, you'll have to piece the backing fabric together widthwise or lengthwise in order to cut a piece approximately 4" larger than the quilt top. I press the seam allowances to one side.

3. Lay the backing fabric on a hard, flat surface (such as a table) with the wrong side facing up. Smooth the fabric out until it's taut (but not stretched) and use tape or binder clips to fasten it to the table. Lay the batting on top, smoothing it

out, but not stretching it. Lay the quilt on top of the batting, centering it on the batting and backing fabric.

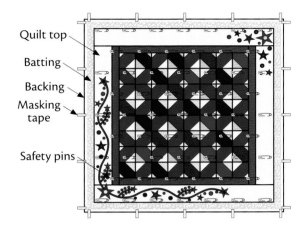

Quilt top
Batting
Backing
Masking tape
Safety pins

4. Pin through all layers using safety pins and spacing them approximately 4" apart over the entire quilt.

5. For machine quilting straight lines, or for ditch work, I recommend using a walking foot. For free-motion quilting, drop the feed dogs and attach the darning foot; this will allow you to quilt curved designs such as stippling or feathers.

6. When all of the machine quilting is finished and the safety pins have been removed, spread the quilt out flat onto the floor and spray it with water in order to remove the water-soluble markings. Don't attempt to remove the markings in the washing machine before you sew on the binding!

7. After the quilt is dry, trim the batting and backing even with the quilt top and square up the corners.

MAKING A HANGING SLEEVE

I recommend making a hanging sleeve for every project. It takes very little time and is much easier to sew onto the quilt as you're finishing it, rather than later on down the road. You never know when you might decide to enter it in a quilt show or take it off of the bed and hang it on a wall. I have a designated "quilt wall" in three rooms in my home. It's fun to change them every few months, depending on the season.

1. Cut a 7"-wide strip of backing fabric the length of the top edge of the quilt, less 2". Double fold a ½" hem at each end and stitch in place. Press in half lengthwise with wrong sides together, aligning the raw edges.

2. On the back of the quilt, center and align the raw edges of the sleeve along the top edge of the quilt. Pin or baste in place. After the binding is sewn to the quilt, whipstitch the folded edge of the sleeve to the backing fabric.

BINDING THE QUILT

All of the binding strips for the projects in this book are based on 2"-wide strips. My preference is for a narrow binding, with the exception of flannel quilts. If you prefer a wider binding, cut your binding strips 2¼" or 2½" wide. Measure the entire perimeter of the quilt and add about 10". Divide this number by 40" to get the number of binding strips you will need to cut for your quilt.

1. Sew together binding strips end to end at a 45° angle, trimming and pressing the seam allowances open. Cut one end of this long binding strip at a 45° angle, fold over ¼" and press. Fold the long binding strip in half lengthwise, wrong sides together, and press.

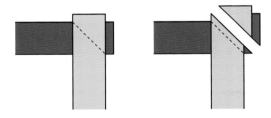

2. Align the raw edges of the binding strip with the raw edges of the quilt top, beginning with the 45° end of the binding strip. Using a ¼" seam allowance, begin sewing approximately 4" from the end of the binding strip and continue until you're ¼" from the corner. Stop stitching and remove the quilt from the machine.

4"

Quilt top

3. Fold the binding up as shown to create a 45° angle. Then fold the binding down to align the raw edges with the next side of the quilt. Begin sewing at the fold and continue to the next corner. Repeat the mitering process at each corner.

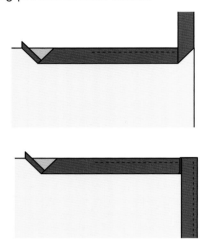

4. When you're nearing the binding tail where you started, trim the binding strip at a 45° angle so that the end of the binding will overlap the beginning of the binding by 2". Tuck the newly trimmed end into the turned-under end, align the raw edges, and continue sewing until you've stitched over the first few stitches.

5. Turn the folded edge of the binding over the seam allowance to the back of the quilt and stitch in place by hand.

MAKING CREATIVE QUILT LABELS

I've tried using many different types of quilt labels: preprinted labels sold on the bolt, packaged muslin label sheets, and traced designs from books. There were times when none of them were what I wanted, and I was usually unhappy with my handwriting! So, I started playing around with freezer paper and using my computer and inkjet printer to make my labels. One thing led to another, and now I look forward to creating a custom label for all of the quilts I make. This is how I do it.

Note: This method is to be used with an inkjet printer only—laser printers could be damaged by the combination of heat and freezer paper.

1. On the computer, center and type the information you want to appear on your label, such as the name of the quilt, the size, who made it, the city, and the date, etc. Choose a font you like, but bolder type will show up the best on your label.

2. Iron the fabric you want to use for the label onto the shiny side of an 8½" x 11" sheet of freezer paper. (The precut freezer-paper sheets work best.) Place the freezer-paper sheet into your printer so that when it feeds through the printer, the label information will print onto the fabric side. Print the label.

3. Peel back the fabric from the freezer-paper sheet and heat set the ink with a hot, dry iron, or use a commercial solution such as Bubble Jet Set to set the ink into the label. The solution is highly recommended if you use colored ink. It's available at many quilt shops and online.

4. Trim the label fabric and add borders 1" to 1½" wide using leftover fabric from the quilt. If you've used fabrics from a specific fabric line, you might want to cut a strip of selvage that shows the name of the fabric designer, the name of the fabric line, and the fabric company, and include that in the border of the label. Another option is to add appliqué that was used in the quilt. You might also insert a ¼" flange that frames the label prior to adding a border. These are just a few ideas . . . be creative and add your own personal touches!

5. Turn under the raw edges of the label approximately ¼" and press. Position the label near one of the bottom corners on the back of the quilt and pin in place. Hand stitch to the backing fabric around all four sides of the label.

Blooms FOR ANNABELLE

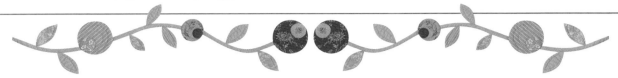

Finished quilt: 71½" x 81" ✳ Finished block: 8" x 8"

This quilt has very special meaning to me, as it was my first Bloom Creek pattern, my first experience with precut 5" Charm Packs, and it was designed with a dear friend in mind. It provided me the opportunity to turn my passion for quilting into a successful business that's been more fulfilling and exciting than I could ever have imagined!

While this design is a good fit for Charm Squares, I converted the Charm Squares of the original pattern to fat quarters and yardage and increased the size substantially. I recommend the freezer-paper-appliqué method (page 9) and invisible-machine-appliqué stitch for a more finished appearance.

MATERIALS
Yardage is based on 42"-wide fabric.

3⅜ yards of light small-scale print for blocks and sashing

1⅝ yards of red-and-gray print for outer border

1½ yards of gray solid fabric for vines, leaves, inner border, and binding

6 fat quarters of assorted red prints for blocks and flowers (or 55 Charm Squares)

6 fat quarters of assorted gray prints for blocks and flowers (or 55 Charm Squares)

4⅞ yards of fabric for backing

76" x 86" piece of batting

Freezer paper

9½" square ruler

CUTTING
Use the patterns on page 21 to cut and prepare the appliqués, referring to "Freezer-Paper Appliqué" on page 9.

From the light small-scale print, cut:
11 strips, 5" x 42"; crosscut into 84 squares, 5" x 5"

25 strips, 2" x 42"; crosscut 12 strips into 48 rectangles, 2" x 8½"

From *each* of the fat quarters of assorted red prints, cut:
7 squares, 5" x 5" (42 total)

From *each* of the fat quarters of assorted gray prints, cut:
7 squares, 5" x 5" (42 total)

From the gray solid fabric, cut:
7 strips, 1" x 42"

8 strips, 2" x 42"

1½"-wide bias strips to total 200" of bias vine

From the red-and-gray print, cut:

8 strips, 6½" x 42"

From the remainder of the fat quarters of assorted red prints, cut:

9 large flowers

9 small flower centers

From the remainder of the fat quarters of assorted gray prints and gray solid fabric, cut:

9 small flowers

9 large flower centers

18 large leaves

18 medium leaves

10 small leaves

MAKING THE BLOCKS

1. Draw a diagonal line on the wrong side of each of the light print 5" squares. With right sides together, place one light square on top of each of the red and gray 5" squares and sew ¼" on each side of the drawn line. Cut apart on the drawn line to make a total of 168 half-square-triangles units. Press the seam allowances of the red units toward the red fabrics. Press the seam allowances of the gray units toward the light print. Doing this allows your seams to nestle together nicely when you sew the blocks together. Square up each half-square-triangle unit to 4½" x 4½". (Refer to "Half-Square-Triangle Units" on page 12.)

Make 84.   Make 84.

2. Each block will consist of two red and two gray half-square-triangles units. Sew blocks together as shown, pressing seam allowances in the direction of the arrows. Make 42 blocks.

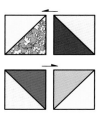 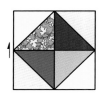

Make 42.

QUILT TOP ASSEMBLY

1. Arrange the blocks in six vertical rows of seven blocks each. Sew a light print 2" x 8½" sashing rectangle to the top of each block, pressing seam allowances toward the sashing. Sew a sashing rectangle to the bottom of the last block in each vertical row. Sew the blocks into rows.

2. Sew the light print 2" x 42" strips together end to end and from this long strip, cut seven 68½"-long strips. (Measure your vertical rows before cutting, and adjust the length of the strips if needed.) Sew the sashing strips to the vertical rows in three sections as shown and press seam allowances toward the sashing.

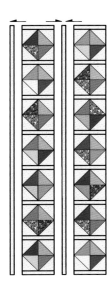 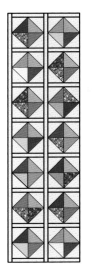 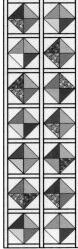

Make 2.   Make 1.

3. Refer to "Bias Vines" on page 11 to make the vines from the bias strips. Position the vines down the sashing strip between each of the block rows, curving them as shown in the photograph on page 18. Apply a few drops of appliqué glue to the wrong side of the vine and press down with your fingers to hold it in place. Add the flowers and leaves in the same manner using the quilt photo for placement guidance, or arrange them to your liking. Hand or machine appliqué everything in place.

4. Sew the three sections together and press.

ADDING THE BORDERS

1. Sew the gray 1" x 42" strips together end to end and cut two 59"-long strips for the top and bottom inner borders. Sew these strips to the quilt, pressing the seam allowances toward the border. Cut two side borders 69½" long and sew them to the sides of the quilt. (You may want to measure your quilt first and adjust the lengths of these strips as needed to fit.)

2. Sew the red-and-gray print 6½" x 42" strips together end to end, cut two 60"-long strips, and sew them to the top and bottom of the quilt, pressing seam allowances toward the outer border. For the side borders, cut two 81½"-long strips and sew them to the sides of the quilt. (You may want to measure your quilt first and adjust lengths as needed.)

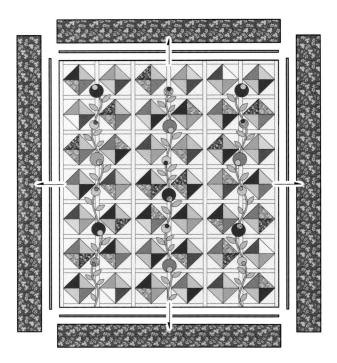

FINISHING

Refer to "Preparing for Machine Quilting" on page 12 for details on marking, layering, basting, and quilting your project. Then use the gray 2"-wide strips to bind the quilt, referring to "Binding the Quilt" on page 13.

Patterns do not include
seam allowances.

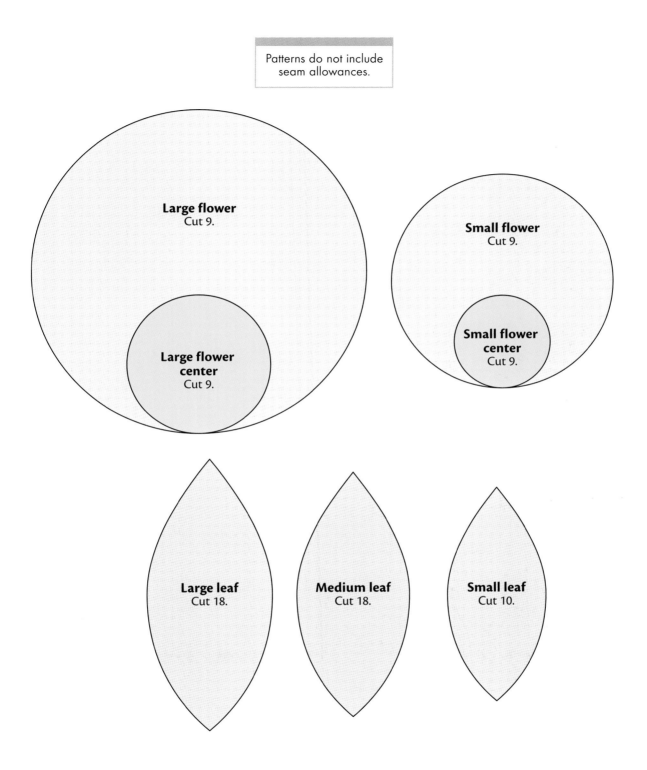

Large flower
Cut 9.

**Large flower
center**
Cut 9.

Small flower
Cut 9.

**Small flower
center**
Cut 9.

Large leaf
Cut 18.

Medium leaf
Cut 18.

Small leaf
Cut 10.

Bloom PILLOW

Finished size: 19" x 19", plus a 2" flange

After I made the Blooms for Annabelle quilt, I immediately knew I wanted to make an accent pillow to use on either the bed or a side chair. Because it can sometimes be difficult to find ready-made accent pillows that will work well with the fabrics used in a quilt, I find making my own is the best solution. This pillow project is simple, yet adds a great finishing touch to accompany the quilt.

MATERIALS

Yardage is based on 42"-wide fabric.

1⅛ yards of gray fabric for pillow front, back, and appliqué

2 fat quarters of red solid fabrics for pillow front and appliqué*

2 fat quarters of light solid fabrics for pillow front

Scraps of red print and gray print for appliqués

20" x 20" pillow form

Freezer paper

I used two different red solid fabrics; one is a bit darker than the other.

CUTTING

Use the patterns on page 25 to cut and prepare the appliqués, referring to "Freezer-Paper Appliqué" on page 9.

From *each* of the fat quarters of red solid fabrics, cut:
1 square, 10½" x 10½" (2 total)

2 squares, 2½" x 2½" (4 total)

From *each* of the fat quarters of light solid fabrics, cut:
1 square, 10½" x 10½" (2 total)

From the gray fabric, cut:
4 rectangles, 2½" x 19½"

2 rectangles, 14½" x 23½"

From the remaining gray fabric, cut:
1 stem

1 flower center B

From the remaining darker red solid fabric, cut:
1 flower center C

From the scraps of red print, cut:
1 flower A

From the scraps of gray print, cut:
2 leaves

MAKING THE PILLOW FRONT

1. Draw a diagonal line on the wrong side of the light 10½" squares. Refer to "Half-Square-Triangle Units" on page 12 to make four half-square-triangle units using the light and red 10½" squares. Press and square up the block to measure 10" x 10". Sew the four half-square-triangle units together as shown.

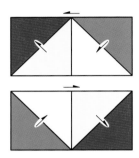

2. Appliqué the flower, flower centers, leaves, and stem in place by hand or machine, referring to "Freezer-Paper Appliqué" on page 9.

3. Sew gray 2½" x 19½" rectangles to the top and bottom of the flower block, pressing seam allowances toward the gray rectangles. Sew a red 2½" square to each end of the remaining two gray rectangles and sew them to the sides of the pillow front.

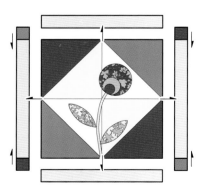

FINISHING THE PILLOW

1. Hem one 23½" side of each of the two pillow backs by pressing ½" toward the wrong side; fold and press ½" again. Topstitch ¼" from the folded edge.

2. With right sides together, lay the pillow backs onto the pillow front, overlapping the back pieces to fit the pillow front. Sew around all four sides using a ¼" seam allowance and turn right side out.

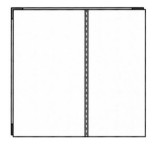

3. On the pillow front, stitch in the ditch at the border seam to create a 2" flange. Insert the 20" x 20" pillow form.

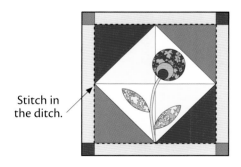

Stitch in the ditch.

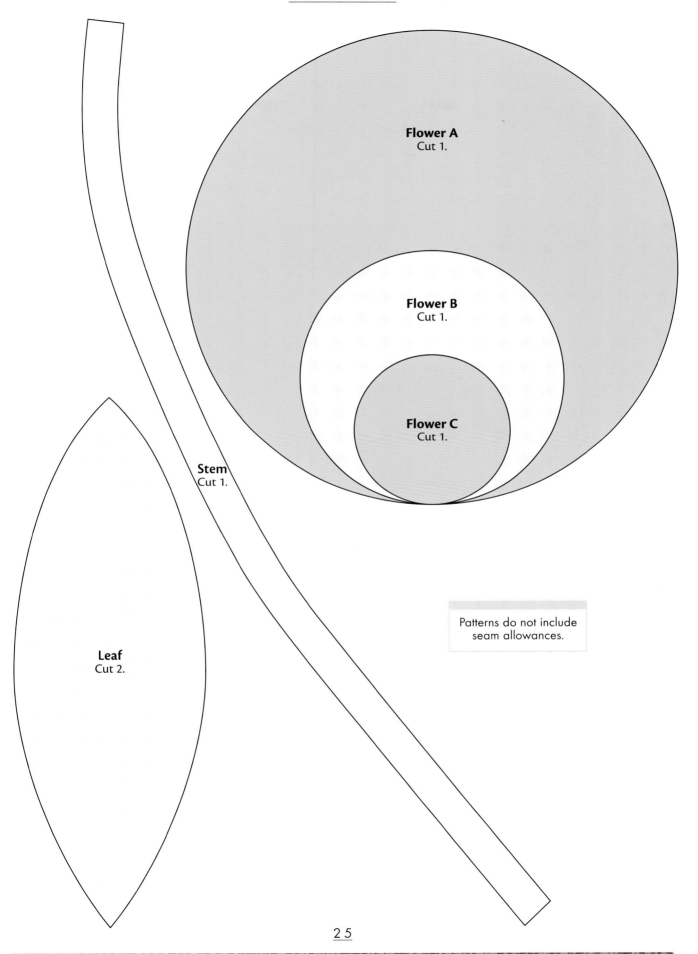

Flower A
Cut 1.

Flower B
Cut 1.

Flower C
Cut 1.

Stem
Cut 1.

Patterns do not include
seam allowances.

Leaf
Cut 2.

FERNDALE Flora

Finished quilt: 62" x 68"

I originally designed this pattern for 35 precut Jelly Roll strips. For this book, I adapted it to be made from fat quarters. While I was at it, I added a few borders and flowers for a fresh new look. You'll find it's quite easy to assemble when you use freezer-paper appliqué and a nearly invisible machine-appliqué stitch.

MATERIALS

Yardage is based on 42"-wide fabric.

10 fat quarters of assorted prints for flowers, pieced borders, and corner triangles*

2⅛ yards of cream print for background and borders

2⅛ yards of peach large-scale floral for outer border

1½ yards of green dot print for leaves, vines, inner border, and binding

4 yards of fabric for backing

64" x 70" piece of batting

Freezer paper

9½" Bias Square ruler

I used 3 red, 3 peach, 2 pink, and 2 green prints.

CUTTING

Use the patterns on pages 32 and 33 to cut and prepare the appliqués, referring to "Freezer-Paper Appliqué" on page 9.

From the cream print, cut:
2 strips, 4½" x 40½"

2 strips, 4½" x 34½"

2 strips, 4½" x 24½"

2 strips, 4½" x 18½"

7 strips, 2½" x 42"; cut each strip in half to yield 14 strips, 2½" x 21"

1 rectangle, 10½" x 12½"

4 squares, 9" x 9"

3 squares, 2½" x 2½"

From *1* of the fat quarters of red prints, cut:
1 basket and 1 handle

From another of the fat quarters of red prints, cut:
2 squares, 9" x 9"

From *1* of the fat quarters of peach prints, cut:
2 squares, 9" x 9"

From the remaining fat quarters of assorted prints, cut:
A *total* of 42 rectangles, 2½" x 4½"
A *total* of 14 strips, 2½" x 21"
A *total* of 3 assorted squares, 2½" x 2½"

From the green dot print, cut:
6 strips, 1½" x 42"
7 strips, 2" x 42"
1⅝"-wide bias strips to total 250" of bias vine

From the remainder of the fat quarters of assorted prints and green dot print, cut:
95 leaves
1 tulip and 1 tulip center
9 dogwood flowers and dogwood-flower centers
1 pansy and pansy center
2 basket knobs and knob centers

From the peach large-scale floral, cut *on the lengthwise grain:*
4 strips, 5½" x 72"

MAKING THE QUILT CENTER

1. Sew each of the 2½" x 21" assorted print strips to a 2½" x 21" cream print strip, pressing the seam allowances toward the assorted prints. Crosscut at 2½" intervals, for a total of 110 two-patch units, measuring 2½" x 4½".

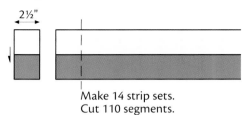

Make 14 strip sets.
Cut 110 segments.

2. Place the prepared basket, handle, knobs, knob centers, flowers and leaves onto the 10½" x 12½" cream print rectangle. Once you're satisfied with the placement, apply a few drops of appliqué glue to the seam allowance of each piece and, with your fingers, press each piece in place. Machine or hand appliqué around each piece. (Refer to "Freezer-Paper Appliqué" on page 9 for more details.)

3. Sew together six two-patch units and three additional 2½" assorted print and cream print squares as shown to make checkerboard borders for the top and bottom of the basket unit. Sew the borders to the basket unit, pressing the seam allowances in the direction indicated by the arrows.

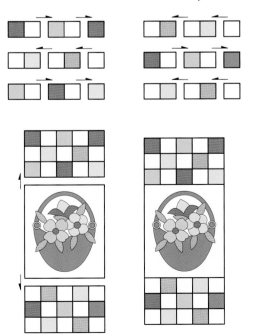

4. Sew together 12 two-patch units for each checkerboard side border and sew them to the basket unit. Press.

MAKING THE VINE AND RECTANGLE BORDERS

1. Refer to "Bias Vines" on page 11 to make the bias vine using the 1⅝"-wide bias strips.

2. Center a bias vine on each of the 4½" x 40½", 4½" x 34½", 4½" x 24½", and 4½" x 18½" cream print rectangles, referring to the vine placement guide on page 32 for the approximate curve. Apply a few drops of appliqué glue onto the wrong side of the vine and press in place as you move along the rectangle. Evenly space leaves on each vine, referring to the quilt photo on page 28 for guidance and glue them in place. Hand or machine appliqué the vine and each of the leaves.

3. Sew together nine 2½" x 4½" assorted print rectangles along their long edges. Repeat to make two. Sew each border to a 4½" x 18½" vine rectangle. Sew the completed borders to the top and bottom of the basket unit, with the vine portion facing the inner checkerboard border.

4. Draw a diagonal line on the *wrong side* of each 9" cream print square. With right sides together, place a 9" cream print square on top of each of the 9" red and peach squares and stitch ¼" on each side of the diagonal lines. Cut apart on the drawn line and press the seam allowances toward the red or peach fabric. Make eight of these half-square-triangle units; square them up to 8½" x 8½". (Refer to "Half-Square-Triangle Units," page 12.)

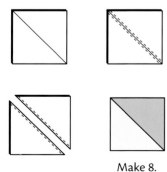

Make 8.

MAKING THE WELCOME UNIT

1. Center each letter onto an assorted light print 4½" square and fuse in place. (Refer to "Fusible Appliqué" on page 10.)

2. With right sides facing, sew the seven letter units together to make the Welcome unit. Press all seam allowances toward the bottom. The unit should measure 4½" x 28½".

3. Sew together 14 assorted 2½" squares and press the seam allowances toward the top. Sew them to the right side of the Welcome unit and press the seam allowances toward the small squares.

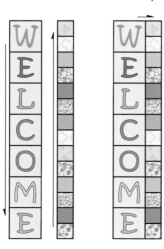

MAKING THE BIRDHOUSE BLOCKS

1. With right sides facing, layer a light print 4" square onto each of the three assorted 4" roof squares and prepare half-square-triangle units as described in "Half-Square-Triangle Units" on page 12. Press seam allowances toward the medium/dark print on one and toward the light print on the other. This will allow the seams to nestle together nicely when the blocks are sewn together. Make six and square them up to 3½" x 3½". Sew two half-square-triangle units together for each roof.

  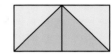

Make 3.

2. With right sides together, sew a light print 1½" x 5" rectangle to each side of the 4½" x 5" birdhouse rectangles. Stitch a light print 1" x 6½" rectangle to the bottom of each birdhouse. Stitch the roof unit to the top of each birdhouse.

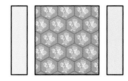 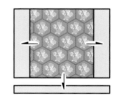

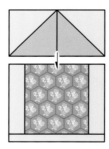 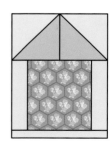

Make 3.

3. Position a birdhouse hole approximately 1¾" up from the bottom, or as desired. Add the perch and machine appliqué in place on each of the birdhouse blocks. Sew the three Birdhouse blocks together.

4. Sew six assorted 2½" squares together and sew to the bottom of the birdhouse unit. Sew the Welcome unit to the birdhouse unit.

FINISHING

Refer to "Preparing for Machine Quilting" on page 12 for details on marking, layering, basting, and quilting your project. Then use the 2"-wide strips to bind the quilt, referring to "Binding the Quilt" on page 13.

Patterns do not include seam allowances and are reversed for fusible appliqué.

Perch
Cut 3.

Hole
Cut 3.

Made by Susan Armington
Finished quilt: 50" x 50" ✳ Finished block: 8" x 8"

I've never seen a more beautiful array of birds than when I was visiting a girlfriend in Kentucky! While sitting on the deck in her backyard, we watched the birds as they visited numerous birdhouses and feeders. That memorable visit was the inspiration for this quilt. I designed it for fusible appliqué, but you can choose hand appliqué if you prefer.

MATERIALS

Yardage is based on 42"-wide fabric.

2¼ yards of light print for background

8 fat quarters of assorted prints for birdhouses, blocks, and borders

Scraps of blue fabrics for birds (or 5 Charm Squares)

½ yard of brown floral for binding

3½ yards of fabric for backing

60" x 60" piece of batting

½ yard of lightweight fusible web (12" wide)

Black pearl cotton and an embroidery needle

CUTTING

Use the patterns on page 43 to cut and prepare the appliqués, referring to "Fusible Appliqué" on page 10.

From *each* of the 8 fat quarters of assorted prints, cut:
1 strip, 4½" x 21" strip; crosscut into:

> 1 square, 4½" x 4½" (8 total)

> 1 rectangle, 4½" x 8½" (8 total)

26 squares, 2½" x 2½" (208 total)

From the remainder of the fat quarters of assorted prints, cut a *total* of:

3 squares, 4½" x 4½", and 1 rectangle, 4½" x 8½" (for the tall birdhouse in the center)

2 squares, 3½" x 3½", and 2 rectangles, 3½" x 5½" (for the medium and short birdhouses in the center)

1 rectangle, 1½" x 3½", and 1 rectangle, 1½" x 7½" (for the birdhouse poles)

13 perches

4 squares, 2½" x 2½"

From the light print, cut:

16 strips, 2½" x 42"; crosscut 11 of the strips into:

    48 rectangles, 2½" x 4½"

    48 squares, 2½" x 2½"

    2 rectangles, 2½" x 12½"

    1 rectangle, 2½" x 8½"

    2 rectangles, 2½" x 7½"

    2 rectangles, 2½" x 3½"

2 strips, 1½" x 22½"

2 strips, 1½" x 24½"

2 strips, 1½" x 40½"

2 strips, 1½" x 42½"*

2 strips, 4½" x 42"; crosscut into 16 squares, 4½" x 4½"

4 squares, 3½" x 3½"

4 rectangles, 1½" x 3½"

1 square, 5½" x 5½"

1 rectangle, 5½" x 9½"

13 birdhouse holes

From the scraps of blue fabrics, cut:

5 birds and 4 wings

From the brown floral, cut:

6 strips, 2" x 42"

If your fabric isn't wide enough, you'll need to cut 3 strips and piece them together to get the length needed.

MAKING THE OUTER BIRDHOUSE BLOCKS

1. Draw a diagonal line on the *wrong side* of the 4½" light print squares. With right sides together, lay a 4½" light print square onto each end of the 4½" x 8½" assorted print rectangles. Sew on the drawn line, trim and press seam allowances toward the light print. Make eight of these flying-geese roof units.

 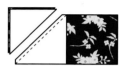

Make 8.

2. Sew a 2½" x 4½" light print rectangle to each side of the eight 4½" assorted print squares. Press seam allowances toward the light print. Sew a roof unit from step 1 to the top of each house unit. Fuse a perch and circle onto each block and machine appliqué in place using a small blanket stitch and thread to match fabric. (Be sure to leave at least ⅜" from the bottom end of the perch and the bottom edge of the birdhouse to allow for seam allowance.)

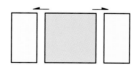 

 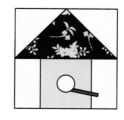

MAKING THE CENTER BLOCK

1. For the tall birdhouse, make a flying-geese roof unit as described in step 1 of "Making the Outer Birdhouse Blocks." Sew three 4½" assorted squares together and add a 2½" x 12½" light print rectangle to each side, pressing seam allowances toward the rectangles. Sew the roof unit to the top and sew a 2½" x 8½" light print rectangle to the top of the roof. The tall birdhouse unit should measure 8½" x 18½".

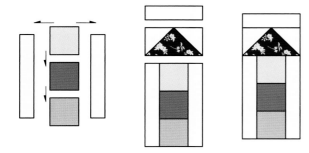

2. Fuse and machine appliqué the holes and perches to the birdhouse using a small blanket stitch and thread to match the fabric.

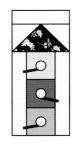

3. For the medium birdhouse, make a roof unit as you did before using a 3½" x 5½" assorted print rectangle and two of the 3½" light print squares. Sew a 1½" x 3½" light print rectangle to each side of a 3½" assorted print square, pressing seam allowances toward the square. Sew this unit to the birdhouse roof.

4. Sew a 2½" x 7½" light print rectangle to each side of the 1½" x 7½" assorted print rectangle. Sew this unit to the bottom of the birdhouse unit. Stitch a 5½" light print square to the top of this

birdhouse unit. Fuse and machine appliqué the hole and perch to the block.

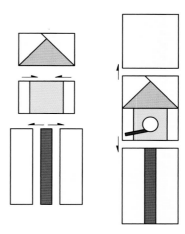

5. For the short birdhouse, make the roof and house units as described in step 3 for the medium birdhouse, using the remaining assorted print rectangle for the roof and the assorted print square for the house. Sew a 2½" x 3½" light print rectangle to each side of the 1½" x 3½" assorted print rectangle and sew to the bottom of the birdhouse. Sew the 5½" x 9½" light print rectangle to the top. Fuse and machine appliqué the hole and perch to the block.

6. Sew the short, medium, and tall birdhouse units together to make the center block measuring 18½" x 18½".

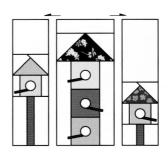

7. Fuse the birds and wings in place and machine appliqué using a small blanket stitch and thread to match fabric. Embroider a French-knot eye as shown onto each of the birds using black pearl cotton.

French knot

41

8. Sew together nine of the 2½" assorted print squares each for the top and bottom borders and sew them to the center block, pressing seam allowances toward patchwork border. Repeat for the sides, sewing together 11 squares for each side. Sew the 1½" x 22½" light print strips to the top and bottom of the center block, pressing in the direction indicated by arrows. Repeat for the sides using the 1½" x 24½" strips.

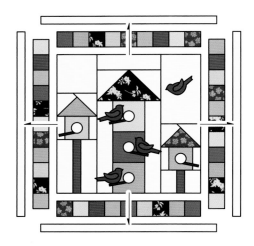

MAKING THE STAR BLOCKS

Each block consists of four flying-geese units, one four-patch unit, and four 2½" light print squares. Press the seam allowances in the direction indicated by the arrows for each step.

1. Make the flying-geese units as described in step 1 of "Making the Outer Birdhouse Blocks" on page 40 using the 2½" assorted print squares and the 2½" x 4½" light print rectangles. Make four flying-geese units with each print for a total of 32.

Make 32.

2. Sew a four-patch unit together using 2½" light print squares and two assorted print squares as shown.

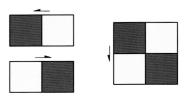

3. Sew the units for the Star block together, as shown. Make a total of eight blocks.

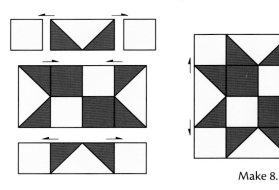

Make 8.

4. Arrange the Star and Birdhouse blocks around the center block, alternating them, as shown. Sew the blocks together in rows for the top, bottom, and sides. Sew the rows to the center block.

5. Sew 1½" x 40½" light print strips to the top and bottom of the quilt. Repeat for the sides, sewing a 42½"-long strip to each side.

ADDING THE BORDERS

1. For the top and bottom patchwork border, sew together 21 assorted print squares for each, and sew them to the quilt. Repeat for the sides, sewing together 23 squares for each side.

2. Sew together the 2½" x 42" light print strips end to end at a 45° angle and cut four 46½"-long strips. Sew a strip each to the top and bottom of the quilt; press seam allowances toward the light print border. Sew a 2½" assorted print square to each end of the remaining two light strips; press toward the strip. Sew the strips to the remaining sides of the quilt. Press.

FINISHING

Refer to "Preparing for Machine Quilting" on page 12 for details on marking, layering, basting, and quilting your project. Then use the 2"-wide brown floral strips to bind the quilt, referring to "Binding the Quilt" on page 13.

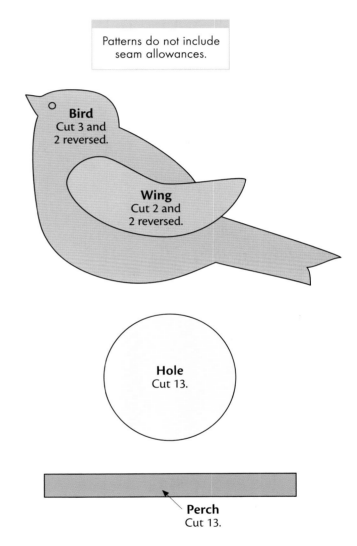

Patterns do not include seam allowances.

Bird
Cut 3 and
2 reversed.

Wing
Cut 2 and
2 reversed.

Hole
Cut 13.

Perch
Cut 13.

"OH" Americana

Made by Susan Armington; quilted by Veronica Nurmi
Finished quilt: 50" x 50" ✳ Finished block: 9" x 9"

The original version of this pattern was designed for precut 5" Charm Squares (approximately 160). I love Americana fabrics and decided to enhance the patriotic feel by adding appliquéd stars and berries on the vine in the border. These blocks go together with ease, and to keep it simple, I used the fusible method of appliqué.

MATERIALS

Yardage is based on 42"-wide fabric

4 fat quarters *each* of red and blue prints for blocks and appliqué

1⅛ yards of small-scale cream print for outer border

⅞ yard of red with cream dot print for inner border and binding

2 fat quarters *each* of cream and tan prints for blocks

½ yard of blue tone-on-tone fabric for bias vine

3 yards of fabric for backing

54" x 54" piece of batting

1 yard of lightweight fusible web (12" wide)

CUTTING

Use the patterns on page 47 to cut and prepare the appliqués, referring to "Fusible Applique" on page 10.

From *each* of the fat quarters of red and blue prints, cut:
8 squares, 5" x 5" (total of 32 red and 32 blue)

From the remainder of the fat quarters of red and blue prints, cut:
2 large stars

6 medium stars

8 small stars

13 large circles

56 small circles

From _each_ of the fat quarters of cream and tan prints, cut:

16 squares, 3½" x 3½" (total of 32 cream and 32 tan)

16 squares, 2" x 2" (total of 32 cream and 32 tan)

From the red with cream dot print, cut:

5 strips, 2½" x 42"

6 binding strips, 2" x 42"

From the blue tone-on-tone fabric, cut:

1½"-wide bias strips to total 110" of bias vine

From the small-scale cream print, cut:

5 strips, 5½" x 42"

MAKING THE BLOCKS

1. Draw a diagonal line from corner to corner on the _wrong side_ of each of the 3½" and 2" cream and tan squares.

2. With right sides together, place a 3½" tan square on the upper-left corner of each 5" blue square. Sew on the drawn line, trim, and press the seam allowances toward the tan fabric. Place a 2" tan square on the lower-right corner of each blue square, sew, trim, and press. Make 32 blue units.

Repeat using the 5" red squares and the 3½" and 2" cream squares. For these units, press seam allowances toward the red fabric.

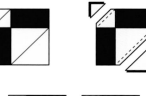

Make 32 of each.

3. Sew two red and two blue units together, pressing seam allowances in the direction indicated by the arrows. Make 16 blocks.

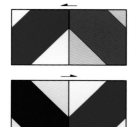
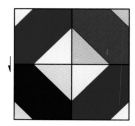

Make 16 of each.

4. Arrange the blocks into four rows of four blocks each. Sew the blocks into rows and sew the rows together, pressing the seam allowances as shown.

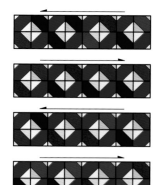
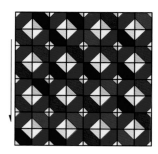

ADDING THE BORDERS

1. For the inner border, cut two of the 2½"-wide red with cream dot strips to 36½" and sew them to the top and bottom of the quilt; press. Sew the remaining three strips together end to end and cut two 40½"-long strips for the side borders. (Depending on the fabric width, you may be able to get a 40½"-long strip from one strip.)

2. Referring to "Bias Vines" on page 11, prepare bias vine using the 1½"-wide blue tone-on-tone bias strips. From this long strip, cut four 5½"-long pieces for the short stems. Cut the remainder of the strip in half.

3. For the outer cream border, sew together 5½"-wide cream print strips as needed to cut two 40½"-long strips for the top and bottom borders and two 50½"-long strips for the side borders. The borders may be sewn to the quilt at this point, or you may choose to appliqué before attaching the borders. If you do this, be sure to leave the two large corner stars off and 5" of bias vine free at the corners until after the borders have been sewn to the quilt.

4. Position the bias vine and short stems first, referring to the photo on page 45 for approximate placement. Apply a few drops of appliqué glue to the wrong side of the vine and press it in place with your fingers, working your way down the border. Add the circles and stars next, and fuse in place. Machine appliqué using matching thread or monofilament.

FINISHING

Refer to "Preparing for Machine Quilting" on page 12 for details on marking, layering, basting, and quilting your project. Then use the 2"-wide red with cream dot strips to bind the quilt, referring to "Binding the Quilt" on page 13.

Patterns do not include seam allowances.

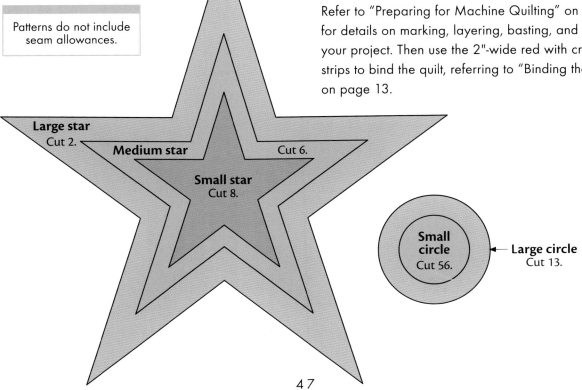

Large star
Cut 2.

Medium star

Cut 6.

Small star
Cut 8.

Small circle
Cut 56.

Large circle
Cut 13.

Finished size: 15½" x 33½" ✳ Finished block size: 4½" x 4½"

This appealing wall hanging or table runner can be made in a day. It's also designed for precut 5" Charm Squares, eliminating half of the cutting time! It could be made using fat quarters, but I like the look with a greater variety of fabrics. Find a fun pack of Charm Squares, or make it from your stash. Either way, with simple piecing and fusible appliqué, it's fun and super easy!

MATERIALS

Yardage is based on 42"-wide fabric.

34 assorted print squares, 5"x 5", for blocks and appliqué*

¼ yard of navy blue-and-red print for border

¼ yard of red fabric for binding

⅔ yard of fabric for backing

20" x 38" piece of batting

⅓ yard of lightweight fusible web (12" wide)

**I used 3 red, 17 light, 6 navy blue, and 8 blue prints.*

CUTTING

Use the pattern on page 51 to cut and prepare the appliqués, referring to "Fusible Appliqué" on page 10.

From 1 of the assorted blue print squares, cut:
1 rectangle, 2¼" x 3¼" (flag block)

From 1 red print square, cut:
2 rectangles, 1½" x 5", and 1 rectangle, 1½" x 2¼" (flag block)

From 1 light print square, cut:
1 rectangle, 1¼" x 5", and 1 rectangle, 1¼" x 2¼" (flag block)

From 5 navy blue print squares, cut:
A total of 20 squares, 2½" x 2½"

From the navy blue-and-red print, cut:
3 strips, 1½" x 42"

From 1 navy blue print square, cut:
1 star

From 2 red print squares, cut:
2 stars

From 3 of the assorted blue print squares, cut:
3 stars

From the red fabric, cut:
3 strips, 2" x 42"

2. Draw a diagonal line from corner to corner on the *wrong side* of each of the navy blue 2½" squares. With right sides together, lay a marked square on one corner of a light 5" square. Stitch on the drawn line, trim, and press the seam allowances toward the blue fabric. Sew a second navy blue 2½" square on the adjacent corner as shown. Repeat to make 10.

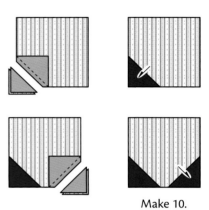

Make 10.

3. Sew four units from step 2, four light 5" squares, and the flag block from step 1 together as shown. Press seam allowances in the direction indicated by the arrows.

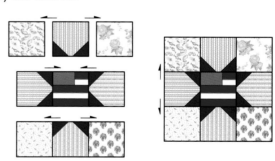

MAKING THE BLOCKS

1. Sew the center flag block together using the red, light, and blue rectangles as shown.

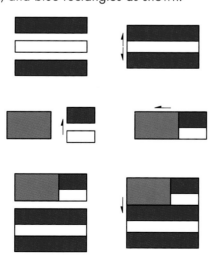

4. Arrange the remaining units from step 2, the blue squares, the light print squares, and the unit from step 3 as shown and sew together, pressing seam allowances in the direction indicated by the arrows.

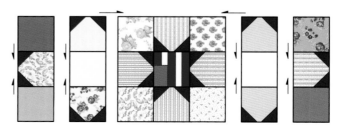

5. From the navy blue-and-red 1½"-wide strips, cut two 14"-long strips for the shorter borders. Stitch to quilt, pressing seam allowances toward the border. Cut two 34"-long strips from the remaining border strips and sew them to the remaining sides of the quilt. (You may wish to measure your quilt before cutting borders and adjust as needed to fit.)

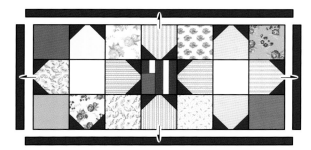

6. Appliqué the stars in place referring to the assembly diagram for placement. (Refer to "Fusible Appliqué" on page 10.)

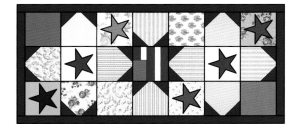

FINISHING

Refer to "Preparing for Machine Quilting" on page 12 for details on marking, layering, basting, and quilting your project. Then use the red 2"-wide strips to bind the quilt, referring to "Binding the Quilt" on page 13.

Pattern does not include seam allowance.

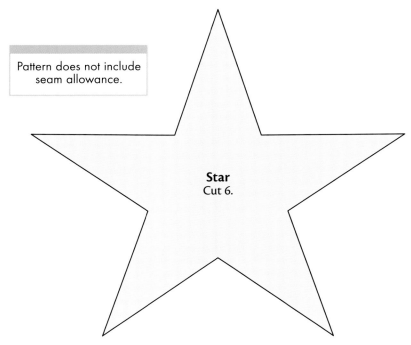

Star
Cut 6.

Brandyvine TOTE BAG

Finished size: 16" x 18" x 4"

Whether you're a quilter or not, a good-sized tote bag can always be put to use. I designed this tote especially with a quilter in mind, making it large enough to hold a quilt in progress, with inside pockets for tools and notions. Simple piecing and beginner-level appliqué make this an easy weekend project. Make this tote with either precut Jelly Roll strips or yardage . . . the choice is yours!

MATERIALS

Yardage is based on 42"-wide fabric.

¼ yard *each* of 7 assorted prints for tote, handles, ties, and appliqués*

½ yard of light print for appliqué background

1 yard of fabric for lining

1¼ yards of medium-weight fusible interfacing (36" wide)

Freezer paper

4" x 16" rectangle of Timtex or other sturdy material for bottom of bag

*Or 19 assorted precut Jelly Roll strips, 2½" x 42"

CUTTING

Use the patterns on page 56 to cut and prepare the appliqués, referring to "Freezer-Paper Appliqué" on page 9.

From light print, cut:
2 rectangles, 6½" x 20½"

From the assorted prints, cut a *total* of:
10 strips, 2½" x 42"

2 strips, 1¼" x 42" (side ties)

4 strips, 1" x 20½" (flanges)

2 strips, 2½" x 36½" (straps)

1 strip, 2½" x 42" (binding)

6 flowers and 6 flower centers

12 leaves

2 vines

From the cream floral, cut:

7 strips, 2½" x 42"

11 strips, 1½" x 42"

From the green diagonally striped print, cut:

12 strips, 1½" x 42"; crosscut into 24 strips, 1½" x 18½"

7 binding strips, 2" x 42"

From the green floral striped fabric, cut:

8 strips, 3½" x 42"

MAKING THE BLOCKS

This quilt is made from two different blocks. Block A uses the various brown 2½"-wide strips and the 6½" squares, while block B uses the 1½"-wide brown strips, the 3½" squares, and the 5" rectangles.

Block A

1. Stitch together 2½"-wide cream floral, brown 2, and brown 3 strips along their long edges as shown. Press the seam allowances toward the darkest fabric. Repeat to make seven of these strip sets. Crosscut the strip sets at 12½" intervals to make a total of 20 strip-pieced rectangles, 6½" x 12½".

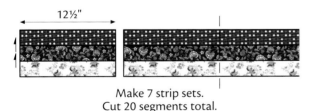

Make 7 strip sets.
Cut 20 segments total.

2. Lay out the units from step 1 with the 6½" brown 1 squares as shown.

3. Begin the block assembly with a partial seaming technique, as follows. With the cream floral side of the strip set adjacent to the 6½" brown square, align the ends of the two pieces and pin. The strip-pieced rectangle will extend beyond the end of the brown square. Sew the rectangle and square together, starting at the end of the pieces and stitching about half the length of the square. Backstitch and cut the threads. Press the seam allowances toward the strip-pieced unit.

4. Working now in a clockwise direction, join the next strip-pieced rectangle to the center square, with the cream floral strip adjacent to the square. This time you can sew the entire length of the rectangle to the center unit. Press as before.

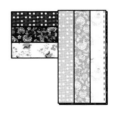 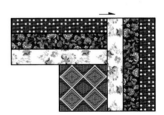

5. Continue in this manner until all four strip-pieced rectangles have been joined to the center square. After joining the last rectangle to the block, go back to the first rectangle and complete the seam. Press. Repeat to make five of Block A. The blocks should measure 18½" x 18½".

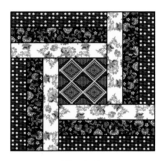

Block A.
Make 5.

Block B

1. Stitch the 1½"-wide cream floral, brown 2, and brown 4 strips together along their long edges to make a strip set. Repeat to make three of these strip sets. Press the seam allowances toward the darkest strips. Crosscut the strip sets at 6½" intervals to make 16 units, 3½" x 6½".

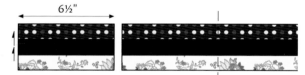

Make 3 strip sets.
Cut 16 segments total.

2. Join the strip-pieced rectangles to the 3½" brown 1 squares, referring to steps 2–5 of Block A. Make four.

Make 4.

3. Stitch 5" x 9½" brown 5 rectangles to the top and bottom of each unit from step 2. Press the seam allowances toward the rectangles. Sew the 5" x 18½" brown 5 rectangles to the sides of each block to complete four of block B.

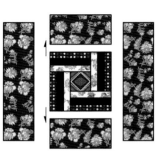 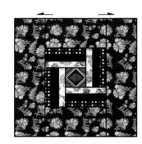

Block B.
Make 4.

QUILT TOP ASSEMBLY

1. Lay out the quilt blocks in three rows of three blocks each, alternating blocks A and B as shown. Position the diagonally striped green sashing strips between the block rows and on the outside of all blocks. Place the brown 2 squares between the sashing strips.

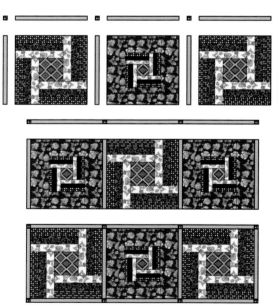

2. Sew the blocks, sashing strips, and sashing squares together in rows. Then sew the rows together. Press all seam allowances toward the sashing strips. The quilt top should measure 58½" x 58½".

3. To make the borders, sew two 1½"-wide cream floral strips together end to end. Likewise, sew together two 3½"-wide green floral striped strips. Sew the white strip to the green strip. Press the seam allowances toward the green strip. Trim this strip set to 62½". Repeat to make a total of four of these border units.

62½"

Make 4.

4. Sew the border units to the quilt top, with the cream floral strips adjoining the quilt center and using the same partial seaming method as used for the quilt blocks. Sew the first unit to the top of the quilt, leaving the last several inches unsewn. Then sew the next border unit to the right-hand side of the quilt. Continue working around the quilt in a clockwise fashion. After joining the last border unit, go back to the first border unit and complete the seam.

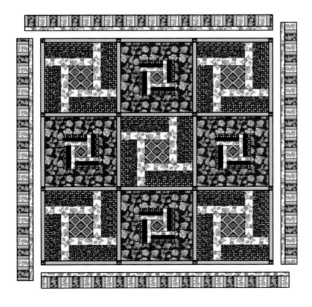

FINISHING

Refer to "Preparing for Machine Quilting" on page 12 for details on marking, layering, basting, and quilting your project. Then use the 2"-wide green diagonal-striped strips to bind the quilt, referring to "Binding the Quilt" on page 13.

A PACK OF *Posies*

Finished quilt: 17" x 51" ❋ Finished block: 6" x 6"

This table runner can be made in no time at all with one charm pack and a half yard of fabric. The flowers and leaves are symmetrical, and the patterns can be used for fusible or hand appliqué. Choose your favorite method and off you go!

MATERIALS

Yardage is based on 42"-wide fabric.

1 charm pack, or 36 assorted blue, green, orange, red, and tan 5" squares, for patchwork blocks and appliqués

½ yard of light print for appliqué background and setting triangles

¼ yard of red print for binding

1½ yards of fabric for backing*

19" x 54" piece of batting

Freezer paper or fusible web

If you don't mind piecing the backing, you can purchase 1⅛ yards.

CUTTING

Use the patterns on page 68 to cut and prepare the appliqués, referring to "Appliqué" on page 8. Set aside 6 light and 6 medium/dark charm squares before cutting.

From the light print, cut:
2 squares, 9¾" x 9¾"; cut into quarters diagonally to yield 8 setting triangles

4 squares, 6½" x 6½"

From *12* medium/dark charm squares, cut:
2 rectangles, 2½" x 4½" (24 total)

From *each of 3* medium/dark charm squares, cut:
4 squares, 2½" x 2½" (12 total)

From *1* green charm square, cut:
4 stems

From *each of 3* green charm squares, cut:
8 leaves (24 total)

From *each of 4 medium/dark charm squares, cut:*
1 large and 1 medium circle (4 total of each)

From *1 medium charm square, cut:*
4 small circles

From the red print, cut:
3 strips, 2" x 42"

MAKING THE BLOCKS

1. Draw a diagonal line on the *wrong side* of the six 5" light squares you've set aside. With right sides together, place one light square on top of each of the 5" medium/dark squares and sew ¼" on each side of the drawn line. Cut apart on the drawn line to make a total of 12 half-square-triangle units. Press the seam allowances toward the darker fabrics. Square up each unit to 4½" x 4½". (Refer to "Half-Square-Triangle Units" on page 12.)

Make 12.

2. Stitch a 2½" x 4½" medium/dark rectangle to a light side of each half-square-triangle unit from step 1 as shown. Press the seam allowances toward the rectangle.

3. Sew a 2½" medium/dark square to one end of each remaining 2½" x 4½" medium/dark rectangle. Press the seam allowances toward the rectangle. Stitch these units to the remaining light side of the units from step 2. Press. Make 12 blocks. Your blocks should measure 6½" x 6½".

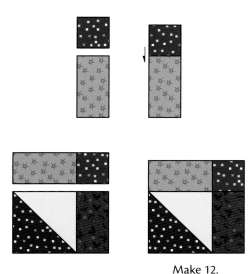

Make 12.

4. Center a prepared stem, six leaves, and a large, medium, and small circle on each of the four 6½" light squares. Appliqué in place by hand or machine.

Make 4.

QUILT TOP ASSEMBLY

1. Lay out the patchwork blocks, appliquéd blocks, and setting triangles as shown above right, so that the flower stems all point toward the center of the quilt. If you want to achieve the same look as the table runner pictured, pay careful attention to the orientation of the patchwork blocks.

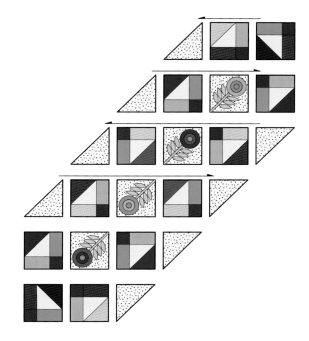

2. Once you're satisfied with the arrangement, sew the blocks and setting triangles together in rows as shown. Press the seam allowances in opposite directions from row to row. Sew the rows together and press.

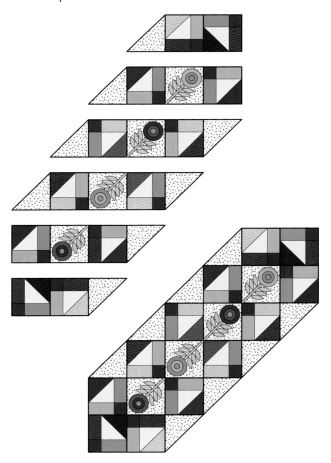

FINISHING

Refer to "Preparing for Machine Quilting" on page 12 for details on marking, layering, basting, and quilting your project. Then use the 2"-wide red strips to bind the quilt, referring to "Binding the Quilt" on page 13.

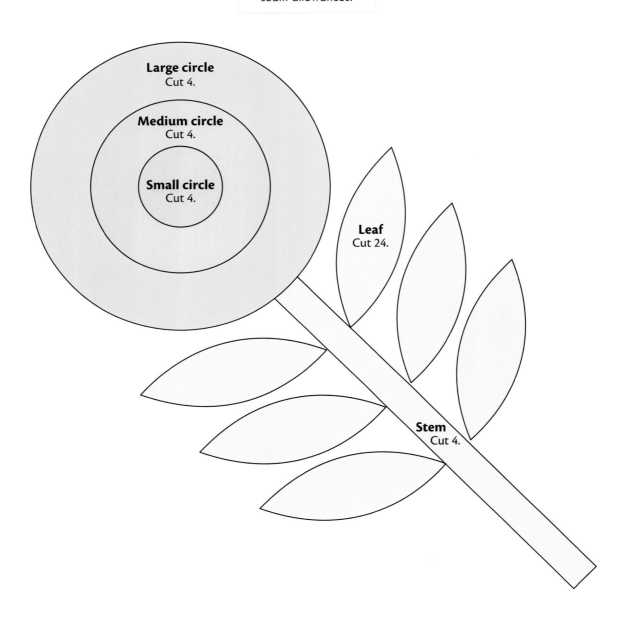

Patterns do not include seam allowances.

Large circle
Cut 4.

Medium circle
Cut 4.

Small circle
Cut 4.

Leaf
Cut 24.

Stem
Cut 4.

Sand DOLLARS

Finished size: 74½" x 80" ✳ Sand Dollar blocks: 4½" x 4½"

Give any room a fresh look by enhancing easy-to-make appliquéd sand dollars with borders of big, beautiful prints. Without any pieced blocks or points to match, this project is suitable for even the beginning quilter. The sand-dollar circles can be appliquéd using either freezer-paper appliqué or fusible appliqué.

MATERIALS

Yardage is based on 42"-wide fabric.

2⅝ yards of cream dot print for Sand Dollar blocks, sashing, and binding

2½ yards of blue-and-brown large-scale floral for borders

1⅜ yards of blue-and-brown large-scale paisley for borders

1 yard of large-scale print for sand-dollar appliqués

⅓ yard of tan tone-on-tone fabric for sashing squares

5 yards of fabric for backing

79" x 84" piece of batting

Freezer paper or 1 yard of lightweight fusible web (36" wide) for appliqué

CUTTING

Use the pattern on page 75 to cut and prepare the appliqués, referring to "Appliqué" on page 8. The sand dollar appliqués in this quilt were cut from different-colored sections of the same large-scale print.

From the cream dot print, cut:
13 strips, 5" x 42; crosscut into:

    38 squares, 5" x 5"

    193 rectangles, 1½" x 5"

8 binding strips, 2" x 42"

From the large-scale print, cut:
38 sand dollars

From the tan tone-on-tone fabric, cut:
6 strips, 1½" x 42"; crosscut into 156 squares, 1½" x 1½"

From the blue-and-brown large-scale paisley, cut:
9 strips, 5" x 42"; crosscut 3 of the strips into:

    2 strips, 5" x 18"

    2 strips, 5" x 32½"

From the blue-and-brown large-scale floral, cut:
5 strips, 5" x 42"

8 strips, 7" x 42"

MAKING THE QUILT CENTER

1. Carefully center a prepared sand dollar onto each of the cream dot 5" squares and appliqué them in place by hand or machine. The sand dollar is very close to the seam allowances, so be sure to keep it centered.

2. Arrange 12 Sand Dollar blocks into four rows of three blocks each, alternating them with cream dot 1½" x 5" rectangles as shown. Sew together and press seam allowances toward the cream dot rectangles.

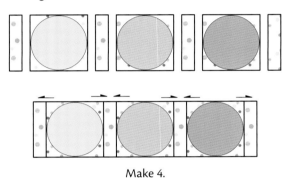

Make 4.

3. Alternating three cream dot 1½" x 5" rectangles and four tan 1½" sashing squares, sew together five sashing strips, pressing seam allowances toward the rectangles.

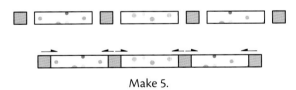

Make 5.

4. Sew the units from steps 2 and 3 together to make the quilt center. It should measure 18" x 23½".

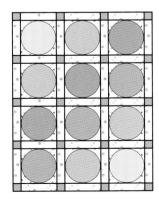

ADDING THE BORDERS

1. Sew paisley 5" x 18" strips to the top and bottom of the quilt center, pressing seam allowances toward the border. Sew a 5" x 32½" strip to each side. Press.

2. Sew together five cream dot 1½" x 5" rectangles and four tan 1½" squares. Make two of these strips and sew them to the top and bottom of the quilt. Make two strips using six cream dot rectangles and seven tan squares each, and sew them to the sides of the quilt, which should now measure 29" x 34½".

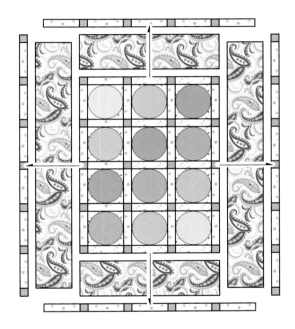

3. Sew together six cream dot 1½" x 5" rectangles and five Sand Dollar blocks; press the seam allowances toward the rectangles. Make two and stitch them to the top and bottom of the quilt. Sew seven rectangles and eight blocks together for each remaining side of the quilt. Sew the strips to the sides of the quilt and press.

4. Make sashing as described in step 2 using seven cream dot rectangles and six tan squares for the top and bottom borders and eight cream dot rectangles and nine tan squares for each side. Sew the strips to the quilt. The quilt should now measure 40" x 45½".

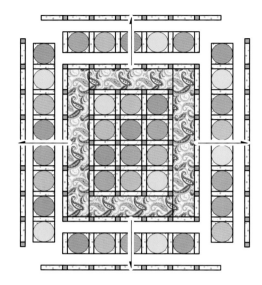

5. Sew large-scale floral 5"-wide strips together end to end and cut two 40"-long strips for the top and bottom borders and two 54½"-long strips for the side borders. Add the borders to the quilt and press.

6. Repeat step 2 using nine cream dot rectangles and eight tan squares for the top and bottom and 10 rectangles and 11 squares for each side. The quilt should now measure 51" x 56½".

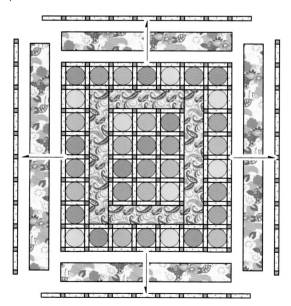

7. Sew paisley 5"-wide strips together end to end and cut two 51"-long strips for the top and bottom borders and two 65½"-long strips for the side borders. Sew the borders to the quilt and press.

8. Repeat step 2 using 11 cream dot rectangles and 10 tan squares for the top and bottom and 12 rectangles and 13 squares for each side.

9. Sew the large-scale floral 7"-wide strips together end to end and cut two 62"-long strips for the top and bottom borders and two 80½"-long strips for the side borders. Sew the borders to the quilt and press. (Before cutting the large-scale floral outer border strips, measure your quilt and cut border strips to fit.)

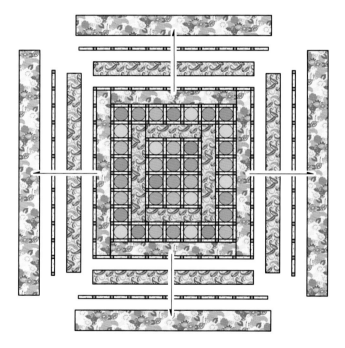

FINISHING

Refer to "Preparing for Machine Quilting" on page 12 for details on marking, layering, basting, and quilting your project. Then use the cream dot 2"-wide strips to bind the quilt, referring to "Binding the Quilt" on page 13.

Pattern does not include
seam allowance.

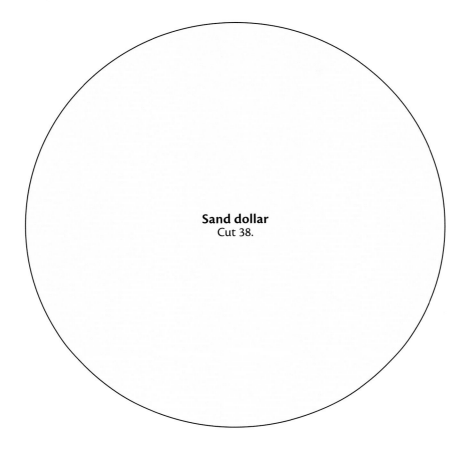

Sand dollar
Cut 38.

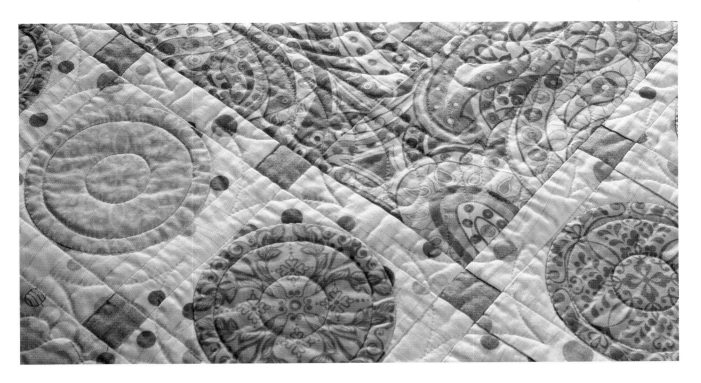

THE *Big* EZ

Finished quilt: 63" x 79" ✷ Finished Four Patch block: 7" x 7"

With big, bold prints so popular right now, I wanted to design a quilt that would feature the prints without having to cut them up and make pieced blocks. Because I'm somewhat of a symmetrical designer, I added a narrow sashing and Four Patch blocks that provide separation and symmetry among the prints. Pick your favorite prints and have some fun with this easy-to-make pattern that gives striking results.

MATERIALS

Yardage is based on 42"-wide fabric.

2 yards of linear oval print for outer border*

2 yards of cream solid fabric for sashing, Four Patch blocks, and binding

1½ yards of a large-scale floral

½ yard *each* of 3 assorted large-scale prints (plaid, paisley, and ovals)

1 blue print and 1 green print fat quarter for the Four Patch blocks and sashing squares

4⅝ yards of fabric for backing

67" x 83" piece of batting

Based on a directional print and lengthwise cutting. For a nondirectional print and crosswise cutting with pieced side borders, 1⅜ yards is enough.

CUTTING

From the cream solid fabric, cut:
21 strips, 1½" x 42"; crosscut into 102 rectangles, 1½" x 7½"

3 strips, 4" x 42"; crosscut each strip in half, for a total of 6 pieces, 4" x 21"

8 binding strips, 2" x 42"

From the blue print fat quarter, cut:
3 strips, 4" x 21"

3 strips, 1½" x 21"; crosscut 32 squares, 1½" x 1½"

From the green print fat quarter, cut:
3 strips, 4" x 21"

2 strips, 1½" x 21"; crosscut into 26 squares, 1½" x 1½"

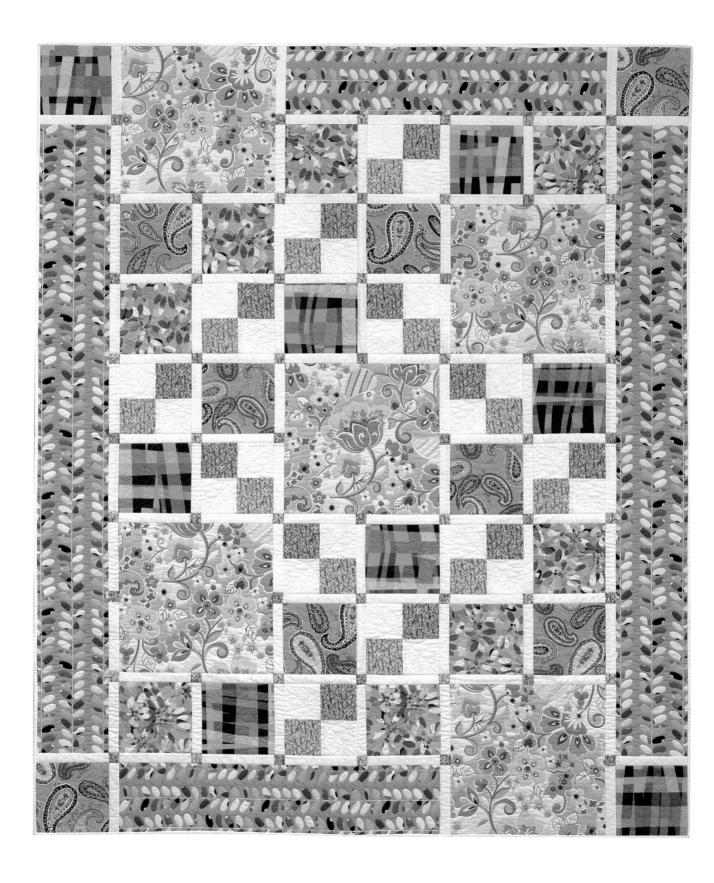

From the large-scale floral, cut:

3 strips, 15½" x 42"; crosscut into 5 squares, 15½" x 15½"

From *each* of the 3 assorted large-scale prints, cut:

2 strips, 7½" x 42"; crosscut into 8 squares, 7½" x 7½"

From the linear oval print, cut *on the lengthwise grain*:

2 strips, 7½" x 63½"

2 strips, 7½" x 31½"

MAKING THE FOUR PATCH BLOCKS

1. With right sides together, sew a 4" x 21" cream strip to each of the 4" x 21" blue and green strips, pressing seam allowances toward the blue and green fabrics. Crosscut at 4" intervals, for a total of 12 segments, 4" x 7½", of each color.

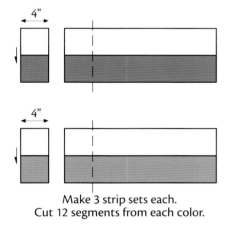

Make 3 strip sets each.
Cut 12 segments from each color.

2. With right sides together, sew a blue and a green segment together to make a Four Patch block, 7½" x 7½". Make 12.

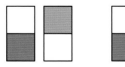

Make 12.

PUTTING THE QUILT TOGETHER

Assemble the quilt in five sections, following the steps and diagrams below. Press after sewing each seam, pressing all seam allowances toward the cream sashing rectangles.

1. **Section A.** Sew together 1½" x 7½" cream sashing rectangles, 1½" blue and green sashing squares, one 15½" large-scale floral square, one 7½" x 31½" linear oval print strip, two 7½" oval print squares, one Four Patch block, and one 7½" plaid square.

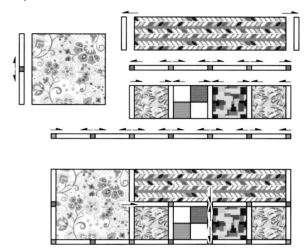

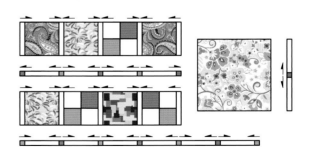

Section A

2. **Section B.** Sew together cream rectangles, blue and green sashing squares, one large-scale floral square, two paisley squares, three Four Patch blocks, two oval print squares, and one plaid square.

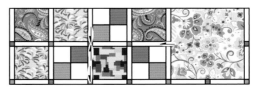

Section B

3. **Section C.** Sew together cream rectangles, blue and green sashing squares, one large-scale floral square, two paisley squares, two plaid squares, and four Four Patch blocks.

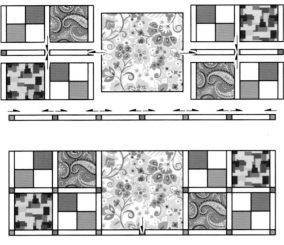

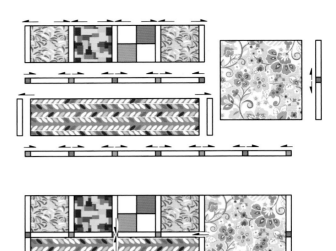

Section C

4. **Section D.** Sew together cream rectangles, blue and green sashing squares, one large-scale floral square, two oval print squares, two paisley squares, one plaid square and three Four Patch blocks.

Section E

6. Sew together sections A through E.

7. Sew a 1½" x 7½" cream rectangle and a paisley square to one end of each of the 7½" x 63½" linear oval print strips. Press. Sew a cream rectangle and a plaid square to the opposite end of each border strip, and sew the border strips to the sides of the quilt.

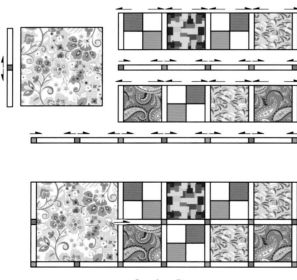

Section D

5. **Section E.** Sew together cream rectangles, blue and green sashing squares, one large-scale floral square, two oval print squares, one plaid square, one Four Patch block and one linear oval print strip, 7½" x 31½".

FINISHING

Refer to "Preparing for Machine Quilting" on page 12 for details on marking, layering, basting, and quilting your project. Then use the 2"-wide cream strips to bind the quilt, referring to "Binding the Quilt" on page 13.

Peppermint PATTIES

Quilted by Veronica Nurmi
Finished size: 44" x 58" ✳ Finished block: 9" x 9"

I've featured an assortment of "mouth-watering" fabrics in one easy-to-make block. The combination of brown, blue, and white prints makes me think of the chocolate and mint combined in one of my favorite candies!

MATERIALS

Yardage is based on 42"-wide fabric.

½ yard *each* of 6 assorted blue and brown prints for blocks

1¼ yards of blue-and-brown print for setting triangles

1 yard of brown with blue polka-dot print for sashing and binding

⅛ yard of diagonally striped fabric for sashing squares

3 yards of fabric for backing

48" x 62" piece of batting

CUTTING

From *each* of the 6 assorted prints, cut:
1 strip, 3½" x 42"; crosscut into:

    3 squares, 3½" x 3½" (18 total)

    6 rectangles, 1½ x 3½" (36 total)

1 strip, 1½" x 42"; crosscut into 6 rectangles, 1½" x 5½" (36 total)

3 strips, 2½ x 42"; crosscut into:

    6 rectangles, 2½" x 5½" (36 total)

    6 rectangles, 2½" x 9½" (36 total)*

From the brown with blue polka-dot print, cut:
12 strips, 1½" x 42"; crosscut into 48 rectangles, 1½" x 9½"

6 binding strips, 2" x 42"

From the diagonally striped fabric, cut:
2 strips, 1½" x 42"; crosscut into 31 squares, 1½" x 1½"

If you want to make four blocks with the same print around the outer edges, as I did (see the light blocks in the quilt photo on page 84), cut 8 rectangles of each size from the chosen fabric. Cut just 4 rectangles of each size from one of the other fabrics.

From the blue-and-brown print, cut:
2 strips, 15½" x 42"; crosscut into 3 squares, 15½" x 15½"; cut each square into quarters diagonally to make 12 side setting triangles (2 are extra)**

2 squares, 8¾" x 8¾"; cut each square in half diagonally, to make 4 corner setting triangles**

**Note that the setting triangles are cut to the size needed; if you want space beyond the block points, cut the squares 17" x 17" and 10½" x 10½".*

MAKING THE BLOCKS

Make the blocks using the precut squares and rectangles from the assorted prints. Use a different print for each step.

1. Sew 1½" x 3½" rectangles to the top and bottom of a contrasting 3½" square, pressing seam allowances toward the rectangles. Using the same print, sew a 1½" x 5½" rectangle to each side of the block.

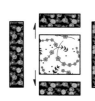

2. Sew a contrasting 2½" x 5½" rectangle each to the top and bottom of the block, followed by a 2½" x 9½" rectangle of the same print to each side.

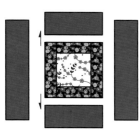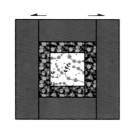

3. Repeat steps 1 and 2 until all of the precut squares and rectangles have been used to make 18 blocks.

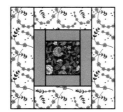

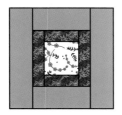

Make 18.

ASSEMBLING THE QUILT

1. Arrange the blocks in diagonal rows alternating them with the brown with blue polka-dot sashing strips and diagonally striped sashing squares. Add the side and corner setting triangles as shown in the quilt diagram.

2. Sew the blocks, sashing strips, sashing squares, and setting triangles in diagonal rows. Sew the rows together and add the corner triangles last.

3. Trim and square up the quilt as needed. Be sure to leave at least ¼" beyond the block points. Leave about 1" if you cut your triangles oversized.

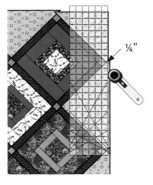

FINISHING

Refer to "Preparing for Machine Quilting" on page 12 for details on marking, layering, basting, and quilting your project. Then use the 2"-wide brown with blue polka-dot strips to bind the quilt, referring to "Binding the Quilt" on page 13.

HOME FOR THE *Holidays*

Finished quilt: 68" x 74" ✳ Finished border blocks: 6" x 6"

Stunning cardinals at rest in a primitive tree, with the addition of holiday blocks and borders, create a festive feeling. For a smaller, faster project, eliminate the outer borders; the tree block framed in red makes a beautiful wall hanging! Use either fusible appliqué or freezer-paper appliqué.

MATERIALS

Yardage is based on 42"-wide fabric.

1⅔ yards of red paisley for borders 1, 3, 5, and appliqué

1⅓ yards of red striped fabric for tree pot, Pinwheel blocks, and binding

1 yard of light pin dot fabric for quilt center and O blocks

⅞ yard of large-scale green floral for outer border 6

⅞ yard of light large-scale floral for border 2

⅝ yard of light print for quilt center and small Pinwheel blocks

½ yard of cardinal print for O blocks and corner blocks*

½ yard of red pin dot fabric for Pinwheel blocks, corner blocks, tree pot, and appliqué

½ yard of green-and-red ornament print for O blocks

½ yard of green print for O blocks, tree pot, and leaves

⅜ yard of green pin dot fabric for Pinwheel blocks and corner blocks

¼ yard of green paisley for leaves

¼ yard of brown fabric for tree trunk and branches

6" x 6" scrap of gold fabric for star and bird beaks

3" x 3" scrap of black fabric for bird faces

4½ yards of fabric for backing

72" x 78" piece of batting

1⅓ yards of 12"-wide lightweight fusible web or freezer paper

Yardage allows for fussy-cutting the squares for the block centers.

CUTTING

Use the patterns on pages 94 and 95 to cut and prepare the appliqués, referring to "Appliqué" on page 8.

From the light pin dot fabric, cut:
2 rectangles, 15½" x 16½"

2 squares, 5" x 5"

2 squares, 4½" x 4½"

2 squares, 2½" x 2½"

3 strips, 3" x 42"; crosscut into 32 squares, 3" x 3"

From the light print, cut:
2 rectangles, 15½" x 16½"

8 squares, 3" x 3"

From the brown fabric, cut:
1 trunk, ½" x 24"

2 each of branch patterns A–E

From the green print, cut:
2 strips, 2½" x 42"; crosscut into 32 squares, 2½" x 2½"

16 squares, 3" x 3"

2 rectangles, 1" x 8½"

20 leaves

From the green paisley, cut:
20 leaves

From the red paisley, cut:
5 strips, 2½" x 42"

2 strips, 2½" x 32½"

2 strips, 2½" x 42½"*

2 squares, 8½" x 8½"

4 squares, 5" x 5"

2 squares, 4½" x 4½"

7 strips, 1½" x 42"

40 berries

3 birds and 2 wings

From the red pin dot fabric, cut:
2 strips, 4" x 42"; crosscut into 18 squares, 4" x 4"

4 squares, 3" x 3"

1 rectangle, 1½" x 8½"

8 squares, 2½" x 2½"

2 birds and 3 wings

From scraps of gold fabric, cut:
1 star

5 bird beaks

From scraps of black fabric, cut:
5 bird faces

From the green pin dot fabric, cut:
2 strips, 4" x 42"; crosscut into 18 squares, 4" x 4"

4 squares, 3" x 3"

8 squares, 2½" x 2½"

From the red striped fabric, cut:
4 strips, 4" x 42"; crosscut into 36 squares, 4" x 4"

1 rectangle, 6½" x 8½"

8 binding strips, 2" x 42"

From the light large-scale floral, cut:
2 strips, 4½" x 36½"

2 strips, 4½" x 42½"

2 squares, 5" x 5"

From the cardinal print, cut:

16 squares, 2½" x 2½"

4 squares, 6½" x 6½"

From the green-and-red ornament print, cut:

2 strips, 3" x 42"; crosscut into 16 squares, 3" x 3"

2 strips, 2½" x 42"; crosscut into 32 squares, 2½" x 2½"

From the large-scale green floral, cut:

7 strips, 3½" x 42"

If your fabric isn't wide enough, cut 3 strips and piece them to get the needed length.

MAKING THE QUILT CENTER

1. Position the A and B branches onto the 15½" x 16½" light print and light pin dot pieces, placing the A branch 7¼" up from the bottom edge of the fabric, and the B branch 2½" from the bottom edge. Appliqué in place. Add the leaves, spacing them 2¼" apart with the first leaf ⅝" from the raw edge of the fabric and appliqué in place. Center and appliqué a berry in place on each leaf unit.

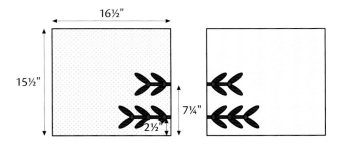

2. Position the C, D, and E branches on the remaining 15½" x 16½" light print and light pin dot pieces, placing the C branch 2¼" down from the top edge of the fabric, the D branch 7" down from the top edge and the E branch 11¾" down

from the top edge. Appliqué the leaves in place with the same approximate spacing as in step 1, followed by the berries.

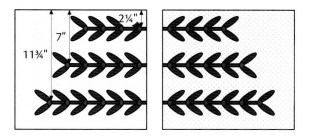

3. Sew the units from steps 1 and 2 together as shown. The center tree unit should now measure 30½" x 32½".

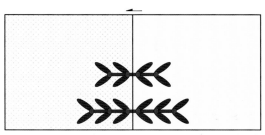

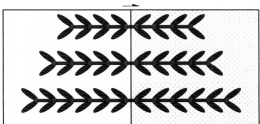

4. Place the 24" trunk over the center seam and appliqué in place. Appliqué the birds and star in place, referring to the photo on page 87 for approximate placement.

5. Draw a diagonal line on the *wrong side* of the two 8½" red paisley squares. Place these squares, right sides together, on the top two corners of the

center tree unit, aligning the raw edges. Sew on the drawn line, trim, and press seam allowances toward the red triangle.

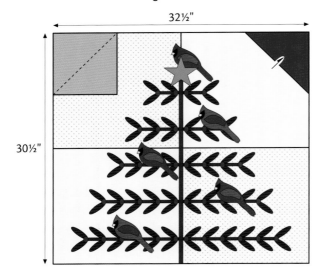

6. Draw a diagonal line on the *wrong side* of the 3" light print squares. With right sides together, lay a light print square onto each of the 3" red pin dot and green pin dot squares. Sew ¼" on both sides of the drawn line. Cut apart on the drawn line and press the seam allowances toward the red or green fabric. Square up the half-square-triangle units to 2½" x 2½". (Refer to "Half-Square-Triangle Units" on page 12.) Make eight red and eight green half-square-triangle units.

Make 8 of each.

7. Sew two green and two red half-square-triangle units together to make a Pinwheel block. Make four blocks.

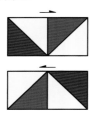

Make 4.

8. Repeat step 6 using two 5" light pin dot and two 5" red paisley squares to make four half-square-triangle units. Square up to 4½" x 4½".

9. Sew a 1" x 8½" green print strip to each side of the 1½" x 8½" red pin dot strip, pressing seam allowances toward the green fabric. Sew this unit to the 6½" x 8½" striped rectangle to make the tree pot.

 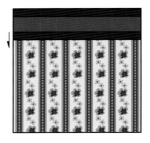

10. Draw a diagonal line on the *wrong side* of the two 2½" light pin dot squares. Place these squares right sides together, on the bottom two corners of the tree-pot unit. Sew on the drawn line, trim, and press seam allowances toward the light print. The tree pot should measure 8½" x 8½".

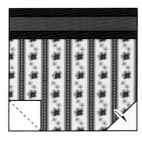 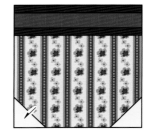

11. Sew together two Pinwheel blocks, two half-square-triangle units, a 4½" light pin dot square, and a 4½" red paisley square. Make two units, one a mirror image of the other as shown.

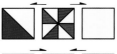 

12. Sew the two units from step 11 to the tree pot. Press.

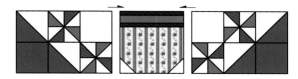

13. Sew the unit from step 12 to the center tree unit, and press seam allowances toward the center tree unit.

ADDING THE BORDERS

1. Sew 2½" x 32½" red paisley strips to the top and bottom of the center tree unit, pressing seam allowances toward the border. Sew a 2½" x 42½" red paisley strip to each side.

2. Sew 4½" x 36½" light large-scale floral strips to the top and bottom of the quilt.

3. For the side borders, make four half-square triangle units with the 5" light large-scale floral squares and the 5" red paisley squares; square up

to 4½" x 4½". Sew one of these to each end of the 4½" x 42½" light large-scale floral strips. Sew the borders to the sides of the quilt.

4. Sew together the remaining 2½"-wide red paisley strips end to end and cut two 44½"-long strips for the top and bottom borders and a 54½"-long strip for each side border.

MAKING THE BORDER BLOCKS

1. Using 16 of the 3" light pin dot squares and the 3" green print squares, make 32 half-square-triangle units and square up the units to 2½" x 2½".

2. Using four of the half-square-triangle units, four 2½" green print squares and one 2½" cardinal print square, sew the block together as shown. Make eight of these O blocks.

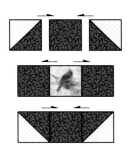 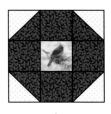

Make 8.

3. Repeat steps 1 and 2 using the remaining 3" light pin dot squares and the 3" green-and-red ornament print squares for the half-square-triangle units, the 2½" green-and-red ornament print squares, and the remaining 2½" cardinal squares. Make 8 of these O blocks, making sure that the ornaments are oriented correctly.

Make 8.

4. With right sides together, lay a 4" red striped square on each of the 4" red pin dot and green pin dot squares and make 72 half-square-triangle units. Always keep the stripe going the same direction when making the half-square-triangle units. Square them up to 3½" x 3½". Sew two red and two green units together to make a Pinwheel block. Make 18 blocks.

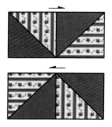
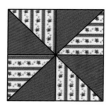

Make 18.

5. Draw a diagonal line on the wrong side of the eight 2½" red pin dot squares and the eight 2½" green pin dot squares. With right sides together, lay a 2½" red pin dot square on two opposite corners of each of the four 6½" cardinal print squares and sew on the drawn line. Trim and press seam allowances toward the red print.

Sew the 2½" green pin dot squares to the remaining two corners on each block to make four corner blocks.

Make 2.   Make 2.

ADDING THE PIECED AND OUTER BORDERS

1. Alternating the Pinwheel and O blocks, sew eight blocks together each for the top and bottom borders. Sew the borders to the quilt and press seam allowances toward the red paisley border. Sew nine blocks together for each side border. Sew corner blocks to both ends of these strips and sew the borders to the sides of the quilt. Press.

2. Sew the 1½"-wide red paisley strips together end to end at a 45° angle and cut two 60½"-long strips for the top and bottom and two 68½"-long strips for the sides. (You may wish to measure the quilt through the center first.) Sew the borders to the quilt, pressing seam allowances toward the red fabric. For the outer border, sew together the 3½"-wide large-scale green floral strips and cut two 62½"-long strips for the top and bottom and two 74½"-long strips for the sides. Add the borders to the quilt top and press.

FINISHING

Refer to "Preparing for Machine Quilting" on page 12 for details on marking, layering, basting, and quilting your project. Then use the 2"-wide red striped strips to bind the quilt, referring to "Binding the Quilt" on page 13.

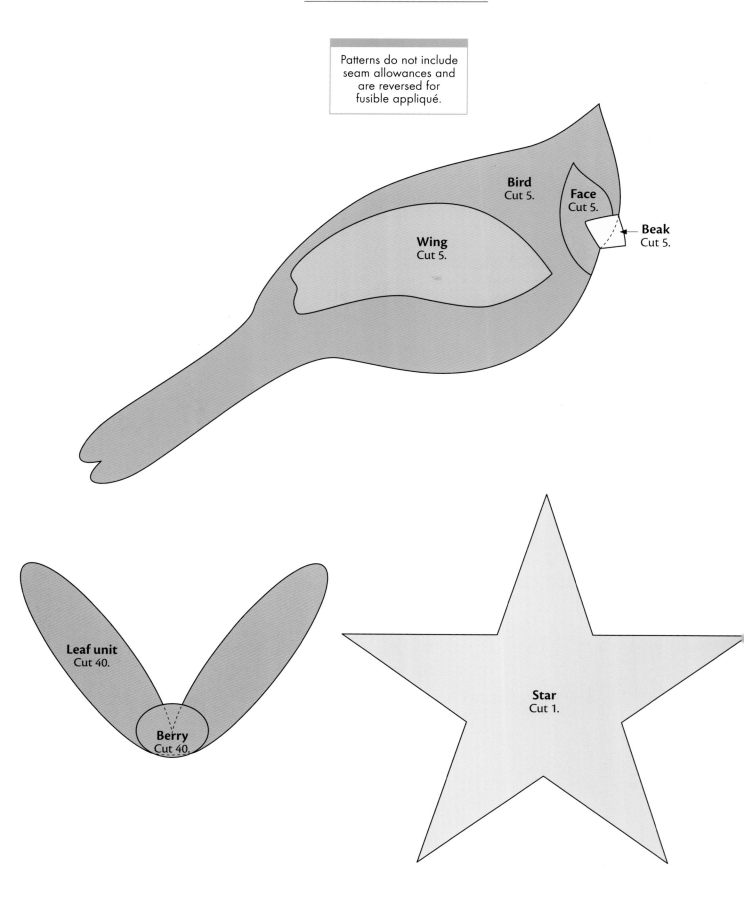

Patterns do not include seam allowances and are reversed for fusible appliqué.

Bird
Cut 5.

Face
Cut 5.

Beak
Cut 5.

Wing
Cut 5.

Leaf unit
Cut 40.

Berry
Cut 40.

Star
Cut 1.

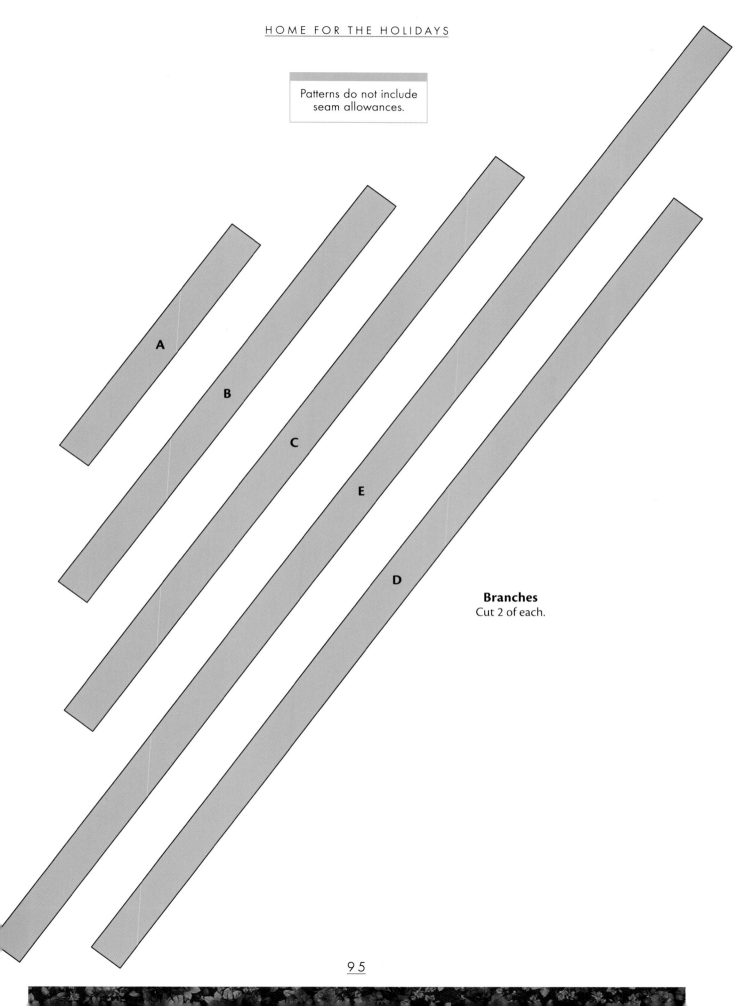

Patterns do not include
seam allowances.

A

B

C

E

D

Branches
Cut 2 of each.

ABOUT THE *Author*

Vicki makes her home in far northern California, in a city known for its extreme summer heat, as well as beautiful rivers, lakes, and mountains. She and her husband enjoy spending their free time in the outdoors and with their four beautiful granddaughters Madilyn, Lexi, Ava, and Olyvia. The oldest two are already becoming avid young quilters!

After taking her first quilting class at a local shop in 1986, she became instantly hooked, making quilt after quilt after quilt. In 2002, she started a machine-quilting business and enjoyed the creativity of the designing involved in machine quilting. With the introduction of precut 5" Charm Packs, she began to dabble in designing patterns specifically for Charm Packs, which ultimately led to starting her pattern design company, Bloom Creek.

Vicki continues to be passionate about her quilting business and now has a wide variety of patterns, with a little something for everyone! Most recently, she has become enamored with English paper piecing and has incorporated that technique into many of her designs.

Vicki strongly believes in personal choices regarding quiltmaking techniques and materials. She would be remiss, however, if she didn't mention that the best choice she has ever made was to marry her high-school sweetheart, Dante, now her husband of 37 years. His never-ending support, encouragement, and patience have afforded her the opportunity to be the crazy, creative, and compulsive quilter that she is today!

There's More Online!

Read Vicki's blog, shop her latest patterns, and sign the guest book at www.bloomcreek.com. Find more great books on quilting at www.martingale-pub.com.